Greek
Drama

Greek Drama

Don Nardo, *Book Editor*

David L. Bender, *Publisher*

Bruno Leone, *Executive Editor*

Bonnie Szumski, *Editorial Director*

David M. Haugen, *Managing Editor*

Greenhaven Press, Inc., San Diego, CA

Library of Congress Cataloging-in-Publication Data

Greek drama / Don Nardo, book editor.
        p.   cm. — (Literary movements and genres)
    Includes bibliographical references and index.
    ISBN 0-7377-0206-0 (pbk. : alk. paper). —
ISBN 0-7377-0207-9 (lib. bdg. : alk. paper)
    1. Greek drama—History and criticism. 2. Theater—
Greece—History. I. Nardo, Don, 1947–   . II. Series.
PA3133.G64   2000
882'.0109—dc21   99-29775
                                                              CIP

Cover photo: Scala/Art Resource, NY

Copyright ©2000 by Greenhaven Press, Inc.
PO Box 289009
San Diego, CA 92198-9009
Printed in the U.S.A.

CONTENTS

Chapter 3: Greek Comedy

those staged by college theater departments.

2. Enduring Fascination for *Oedipus the King*
The story and title character of one Greek drama—*Oedipus the King*, by Sophocles—has, over the course of many centuries, continued to attract, fascinate, and deeply move theatrical producers, actors, audiences, and general readers in diverse nations and cultures.

3. Ancient Greek Drama Is Still Relevant
Modern audiences still relate to many of the ancient Greek plays because the majority of their themes are universal to all times and places. Thus, for example, since the 1960s, when political protest helped to transform many modern societies, audiences readily relate to the title character's bold defiance of the state in Sophocles' *Antigone*.

FOREWORD

The study of literature most often involves focusing on an individual work and uncovering its themes, stylistic conventions, and historical relevance. It is also enlightening to examine multiple works by a single author, identifying similarities and differences among texts and tracing the author's development as an artist.

While the study of individual works and authors is instructive, however, examining groups of authors who shared certain cultural or historical experiences adds a further richness to the study of literature. By focusing on literary movements and genres, readers gain a greater appreciation of influence of historical events and social circumstances on the development of particular literary forms and themes. For example, in the early twentieth century, rapid technological and industrial advances, mass urban migration, World War I, and other events contributed to the emergence of a movement known as American modernism. The dramatic social changes, and the uncertainty they created, were reflected in an increased use of free verse in poetry, the stream-of-consciousness technique in fiction, and a general sense of historical discontinuity and crisis of faith in most of the literature of the era. By focusing on these commonalities, readers attain a more comprehensive picture of the complex interplay of social, economic, political, aesthetic, and philosophical forces and ideas that create the tenor of any era. In the nineteenth-century American romanticism movement, for example, authors shared many ideas concerning the preeminence of the self-reliant individual, the infusion of nature with spiritual significance, and the potential of persons to achieve transcendence via communion with nature. However, despite their commonalities, American romantics often differed significantly in their thematic and stylistic approaches. Walt Whitman celebrated the communal nature of America's open democratic society, while Ralph Waldo

Emerson expressed the need for individuals to pursue their own fulfillment regardless of their fellow citizens. Herman Melville wrote novels in a largely naturalistic style whereas Nathaniel Hawthorne's novels were gothic and allegorical.

Another valuable reason to investigate literary movements and genres lies in their potential to clarify the process of literary evolution. By examining groups of authors, literary trends across time become evident. The reader learns, for instance, how English romanticism was transformed as it crossed the Atlantic to America. The poetry of Lord Byron, William Wordsworth, and John Keats celebrated the restorative potential of rural scenes. The American romantics, writing later in the century, shared their English counterparts' faith in nature; but American authors were more likely to present an ambiguous view of nature as a source of liberation as well as the dwelling place of personal demons. The whale in Melville's *Moby-Dick* and the forests in Hawthorne's novels and stories bear little resemblance to the benign pastoral scenes in Wordsworth's lyric poems.

Each volume in Greenhaven Press's Great Literary Movements and Genres series begins with an introductory essay that places the topic in a historical and literary context. The essays that follow are carefully chosen and edited for ease of comprehension. These essays are arranged into clearly defined chapters that are outlined in a concise annotated table of contents. Finally, a thorough chronology maps out crucial literary milestones of the movement or genre as well as significant social and historical events. Readers will benefit from the structure and coherence that these features lend to material that is often challenging. With Greenhaven's Great Literary Movements and Genres in hand, readers will be better able to comprehend and appreciate the major literary works and their impact on society.

INTRODUCTION

The surviving plays of the great ancient Greek dramatists—most notably Aeschylus, Sophocles, Euripides, and Aristophanes—are still performed today on stages and screens around the world. Their popularity does not rest on trendy curiosity or nostalgia for something old and quaint; nor do producers, directors, and actors stage and re-stage them mainly out of academic interest for the peculiar trappings of a civilization long dead.

CONTINUED MEANING AND RELEVANCE

To the contrary, ancient Greek drama, both tragedy and comedy, lives on because the major themes it explores are as meaningful to modern audiences as they were to ancient ones. As University of Florida scholar Karelisa Hartigan puts it, the message of the works of Aeschylus and his colleagues "has consistently been deemed important because the issues addressed by the writers of fifth-century B.C. Athens continue to be current, continue to have a relevance" for today's world.[1] "Ideas of morality," Hartigan goes on,

> the right of political protest, the quest for self identity, the validity of revenge, the nature of sacrifice and the need for it: the Greek tragedies address all these issues. . . . In the unchanging texts of the ancient Greek playwrights, [modern] directors and producers find a meaning that has validity, a message they can interpret for their audience, for their own society.[2]

The human experience of suffering, so basic to all people in all times and places, constitutes only one of many examples of the universal themes the Greek dramatists, in this case the tragedians, explored. In his *Oedipus the King*, often called the greatest tragedy ever written, Sophocles portrayed the title character's fall from the heights of prosperity and happiness to the depths of wretchedness and despair; and in doing so the playwright showed that suffering is an inevitable part of life and takes the ultimate measure of every person, rich or poor, mighty or humble. "O citizens of our native Thebes, behold," echo the words of the play's finale.

> Here is Oedipus, who . . . became ruler of our city and was regarded with envy by every citizen because of his good fortune. Think of the flood of terrible disaster that has swept over him. Thus, since we are all mortal, consider even a man's final day on earth and do not pronounce him happy until he has crossed the finish line of life without the pain of suffering.[3]

Oedipus's sin was that he had tried to avoid the fate the gods had decreed for him. And Sophocles reminded his audiences of the ultimate folly of any such attempt. Significantly, today's audiences still readily identify with that powerful reminder; for, in the words of the late, great classical scholar C.M. Bowra:

> Modern thought still retains the Greek belief that man's acceptance of his fate, no matter how intolerable that fate may seem, can be ennobling. Greek tragedy provides no explicit answers for the sufferings of humanity, but it exposes them and shows how they happen, and how they may be borne.[4]

NOTES

1. Karelisa V. Hartigan, *Greek Tragedy on the American Stage: Ancient Drama in the Commercial Theater, 1882–1994*. Westport, CT: Greenwood Press, 1995, p. 1.

2. Hartigan, *Greek Tragedy on the American Stage*, p. 153.

3. Quoted in Rhoda A. Hendricks, ed. and trans., *Classical Gods and Heroes: Myths as Told by the Ancient Authors*. New York: Morrow Quill, 1974, p. 152.

4. C.M. Bowra, *Classical Greece*. New York: Time-Life Books, 1965, p. 102.

Drama's Origins and First Great Flowering

The arts of drama and theater as the Western world has come to know them developed and enjoyed their first great flowering in the ancient Greek city-state of Athens in the brief period spanning the late sixth through early fourth centuries B.C. They did not develop in a vacuum, to be sure. During these years Greece, particularly Athens, was the scene of a profound intellectual, artistic, and political revolution in which a handful of supremely gifted individuals created a cultural legacy that has thrilled and inspired the world ever since. "Looking back on those times," noted classicist Rex Warner remarks,

> [we] can see them as a unique period in the history of the world, a period in which were laid the foundations of our present-day civilization. These years saw the invention of drama, the fine flowering of sculpture and architecture, the foundations laid of law and politics, of science and philosophy. But all these were merely aspects of a way of life achieved miraculously, it seems to us who look back on it all, by a few generations of men. In ways unparalleled before in history men sought to understand, to explain and, at least in so far as human relationships were concerned, to reshape the world in which they lived. They looked at everything in heaven and earth with strangely unprejudiced eyes, and from what they saw they made new products of theory, imagination, and behavior.[1]

One of these new products was the theater, in which a new breed of artist—the dramatist—plied his trade.

The Rituals of Dionysus

Although the exact origins of theater and drama are and will likely always remain uncertain, scholars have managed to piece together a likely scenario for their inception. At least by the eighth century B.C., the Greeks had developed elaborate rituals attending worship of the fertility god Dionysus (son of Zeus, leader of the gods). Among these rituals was a kind of poetry and ceremony called the dithyramb. This special form of verse, which the worshipers sang and danced to, eventually became the chief highlight of the religious festivals dedicated to the god. Apparently the dithyramb told the story of Dionysus's life and adventures, as set down in various myths the Greeks had inherited from earlier times.

As time went on, the dithyrambic ceremony expanded to include other gods, as well as human heroes, and took on increasingly dramatic form. A priest and a selected group of worshipers stood in front of the rest of the congregation and, to the accompaniment of flutes, cymbals, and other instruments, enacted a god's or hero's story through song and dance. It would not be an exaggeration, then, to see the priest and his assistants as the first performers and the rest of the congregation as their audience. Another advance occurred when priests began elaborating on and offering their own versions of the accepted story lines; this made them, in a sense, the first playwrights. In fact, this is exactly the way the fourth-century B.C. philosopher-scholar Aristotle believed that drama originated. Tragedy (the first form drama took), he said,

> certainly began in improvisations [spontaneous creations]. . . originating with the authors of the dithyramb . . . which still survive . . . in many of our cities. And its advance [evolution into the art of drama] after that was little by little, through their improving on whatever they had before them at each stage.[2]

Another piece of evidence supporting this scenario for tragedy's origins is that the dithyramb was also called "goat-song" because some of those involved in the ceremony dressed as satyrs (creatures half-man and half-goat). The term "tragedy" most likely developed from the Greek words *tragos,* meaning goat, and *odi,* meaning song.

THESPIS AND THE FIRST PLAYS

Another important source for drama was epic poetry, especially the works of the legendary ninth- or eighth-century B.C. poet Homer. His *Iliad* was the story of the exploits of Achilles and other Greek heroes in the last year of their ten-year siege of Troy; and his *Odyssey* told of the wanderings of one of these heroes, Odysseus, in the years following the siege. At first, bards like Homer merely stood before an audience (probably mainly aristocrats at first) and recited these tales. In time, however, such recitations became more formal and attached to religious festivals. An important turning point came in 566 B.C. when an Athenian leader named Solon, who wanted to enhance the prestige of a popular festival, instituted Homeric recitation contests—the *rhapsodia*. (The performers were known as *rhapsodes*.)

Not long afterward, perhaps about the year 534, Athens instituted a large-scale annual religious festival—the City Dionysia—in Dionysus's honor. The festival featured a dramatic competition involving both formal dithyramb and *rhapsodia*. The contest's first winner was a poet named Thespis, who is credited with transforming these traditional presentations into the first example of what later became recognized as a theatrical play, part of a new art form called tragedy. Thespis's play utilized most of the standard elements of the dithyramb and *rhapsodia* but featured some important innovations. One was the addition of a chorus to the *rhapsodia*. Evidently, the chorus members recited in unison some of the lines and also commented on the events of the story to heighten the dramatic effect. Thespis's other novel idea was to impersonate, rather than just tell about, the story's heroes. In detaching himself from the chorus and playing a character, he became the world's first actor.[5]

In a sense, then, Thespis created the formal art form of theater almost overnight. In setting up regular interplay between himself, the actor, and the chorus, he introduced the basic theatrical convention of dialogue; he also experimented with ways of disguising himself so that he could portray different characters in the same dramatic piece. He eventually decided to don a series of masks, which became another standard convention of Greek theater (and later Roman theater, which borrowed many Greek conventions). In addition, Thespis apparently helped to define the role of the audience. By enlarging the dithyramb into a piece of art and entertainment, he transformed the congregation into a true theater audience. (For these innovations, Thespis became a theater immortal; actors are still called "thespians" in his honor.)

PLAYWRIGHTS AND BACKERS

A number of talented and ambitious writer-actor-managers soon entered the new art form Thespis had introduced and competed with him in the City Dionysia. Among these pioneers were Choerilus, who wrote some 160 plays and won the great dramatic competition thirteen times; and Pratinas, who it was said wrote eighteen tragedies. For subjects, these men relied mainly on the standard Greek myths, as well as on the tales in the *Iliad* and other epics now lost. They also depicted important recent historical events. The popular playwright Phrynichus, for instance, made a stir at the City Dionysia around 492 B.C. for his play *The Fall of Miletus*, about the Persian capture of the most prosperous Greek city in Asia Minor (what is now Turkey). According to the fifth-century B.C. Greek historian Herodotus, the play was so moving that his Athenian audience "burst into tears."[4]

Unfortunately, all of the plays of these early theater giants are lost. However, the survival of a few fragments, as well as descriptions of the plays by later writers, provide a rough idea of how they appeared in performance. According to former University of Southern California scholar James H. Butler:

> In performance, early Greek tragedies consisted of a series of acted episodes performed by one . . . actor who also conversed with the leader of a chorus. During this action, chorus members reacted in patterned movements and gestures to what was happening. . . . Between episodes the chorus danced, recited . . . and sang choral odes [songs] that related to past events or foreshadowed what was about to happen.[5]

Such performances became increasingly elaborate and dramatic, and the City Dionysia festival accordingly developed into a major holiday attraction, eagerly awaited each year by the populace. Covering several days at the end of March, the festival was open to all Greeks; that is, people from other city-states could attend or enter plays in the competition. However, the competition itself, including all play production, remained an Athenian monopoly for a long time to come.

Not surprisingly then, the Athenian government wisely took advantage of the celebration as a showcase for the city's growing wealth and cultural achievements. To this end, the state financed the theater building and its maintenance, paid fees to the actors (and possibly the playwrights), and also provided the prizes for the dramatic contests. All other expenses of play production, including costumes, sets, musicians, and the training of the choruses, were the responsibility of the backers, the *choregoi*, well-to-do citizens whom the state called on to help support the festival. These men were chosen by lot (random drawing) each year and each *choregus* was assigned to a specific playwright.

As for the duties of the playwrights themselves, in addition to writing the plays they usually acted in them, trained the choruses, composed the music, choreographed the dances, and supervised all other aspects of production. In fact, they were so involved in instructing others that at the time they were known as *didaskaliai*, meaning teachers.

THE THEATER, COMPETITIONS, AND AWARDS

Typically, rehearsals lasted for months and continued right up until the opening of the festival. On the first day of the competition, the playwrights, their *choregoi* and choruses, along with important public officials, took part in a stately procession that wound its way through the city streets. The colorful parade ended up in the Theatre of Dionysus, near the southeastern foot of the Acropolis (the stony hill on which a complex of important temples rested).

The earliest version of this world famous theater was constructed in the early 490s B.C. and it underwent a number of periodic renovations and improvements over the course of the following three centuries. (An earlier Athenian theater, the world's first, had been erected three to five decades before; but it had been abandoned after its wooden seating section collapsed in 499, killing several spectators.) By the mid-fifth century B.C., it consisted of a circular "dancing place," the orchestra, where the actors and choruses performed; entrances (*parodoi*) for the performers on two sides of the orchestra; an audience area (*theatron*, the source of the word theater), with wooden (later stone) bleachers accommodating a maximum of some 14,000 people; and a "scene building" (*skene*, the source of the word scene), located in front of and facing the orchestra and *theatron*, a facility that served as a background for the performers and probably contained dressing rooms and storage spaces for stage props.[6]

After the great procession entered the theater, the public sacrifice of a bull to Dionysus took place. Then the competitions started with the dithyrambic contests, a gesture to tradition. Finally, in the days that followed, each of three playwrights presented three tragedies. (Tragedy was still the main dramatic form, as comedy was not yet well developed or popular; when comedies eventually began to be performed at the City Dionysia in 501 B.C., they took place at night, after day-long presentations of tragedy.)

Probably the festival's most eagerly awaited moment was the awards ceremony, in many ways an ancient counterpart to today's Oscar night. The winners were chosen by a panel of ten judges, and the prizes consisted of crowns of ivy, which were awarded to the *choregoi* rather than to the playwrights. The victors also received lavish praise, so it is certain that one of the main incentives for a backer was the knowledge that winning would greatly increase his prestige in the community.

STAGING, MASKS, COSTUMES, AND MECHANICAL DEVICES

The exact criteria the judges used to choose the victors of the festival competitions are unknown. The exact details of the staging and presentation of the plays during Greek drama's golden age in the mid-to-late fifth century B.C. are also uncertain. However, the structure of the plays themselves, along with scenes painted on vases and cups, various ancient literary descriptions, and other evidence, supports the following general reconstruction.

A play began when the actors and chorus, accompanied by a flute player (and perhaps sometimes other musicians) marched through the *parodoi* singing an entrance song (*parodos*). They kept in strict formation, moving and gesturing in unison. Once the chorus members reached their pre-assigned positions in the orchestra and the story began to unfold, they broke formation, moved from place to place, and reacted to the play's characters and events with appropriate verses and gestures. Among the chorus's several possible functions were to ask the characters probing questions and give them advice (both of which illuminated the story's themes); to set the play's overall mood by the tone of its singing and reciting; and to vary the play's rhythm by either slowing down or speeding up their verses.

The actors who engaged in interplay with the chorus wore elaborate masks, usually made of linen stiffened with clay and brightly painted. "The masks worn by the chorus and actors seem to have been fairly standardized," comments noted scholar Bernard M.W. Knox.

> There were recognizable types—old man, middle-aged man, youth, old woman, etc. . . . The masks certainly ruled out the play of facial expression which we regard today as one of the actor's most important skills, but in the Theatre of Dionysus,

where even the front row of spectators was sixty feet away from the stage (the back rows were three hundred feet away), facial expression could not have been seen anyway. And the masks had a practical value. They made it possible for the same actor to play two or even three or four different parts in different scenes of the play.[7]

The masks also made it possible for men to play women's parts, an important and closely-observed convention in ancient Greek theater. The Greeks considered it improper for women to bare their emotions, even staged ones, in public.

Like masks, Greek theatrical costumes were brightly colored. This was partly to catch the eye from a distance, since most of the spectators sat so far from the actors. Also as in the case of masks, costume colors aided in character recognition, as, for example, a queen's gown would be purple, the traditional color of royalty in ancient times. The actors used props, too, as they do today, although the Greeks used them more sparingly. The most common props were chariots, couches, statues of gods, shields and swords, and biers to display dead bodies.

The settings, on the other hand, were left mostly to the audience's imagination. In the fifth and fourth centuries B.C., as a rule the action of the plays took place outdoors, in front of a house, palace, temple, or other familiar structure. The *skene*, redecorated appropriately by the playwright-producer, represented the fronts of these buildings. Interiors could not be shown, and there is no solid evidence for the use of movable painted scenery like that in modern theaters.

As time went on, Greek theatrical producers introduced various mechanical devices to enhance both setting and atmosphere. Perhaps the most common was the *eccyclema*, or "tableau machine." Violent acts were almost always committed "indoors," and therefore offstage and out of sight, and the audience learned about them secondhand from messengers or other characters. Sometimes, however, to achieve shock value, a doorway in the *skene* would open and stagehands would push out the *eccyclema*, a movable platform on rollers. On the platform, frozen in a dramatic, posed tableau, would be both the murderer and the victim, usually depicted in the seconds immediately following the crime. Other mechanical devices included a "lightning machine" (*keraunoskopeion*); "thunder machine" (*bronteion*); and the *machina* (the source of the word machine), a crane with a mechanical arm used to "fly" an actor playing a god or hero through the air above the stage.[8]

THE AUDIENCE

The main goal of Athenian producers in employing the right blend of recitation, singing, dancing, music, masks, costumes, props, machines, and so on, was, of course, to entertain their audiences. That they consistently achieved this goal is shown by the fact that performances in the Theatre of Dionysus in the fifth century B.C. were always sold out. The Athenians, it seems, also invented the theater ticket, a necessity since the number of people who desired entrance far exceeded the facility's seating capacity. As the late scholar of ancient theater Arthur Haigh reminds us, "The audience at the dramatic performances, whether tragic or comic, was drawn from every class of the population. Men, women, boys, and slaves were all allowed to be present."[9] Even many poor people became regulars after the famous democratic leader Pericles instituted a special government fund to subsidize their theater tokens about the year 450 B.C. The tokens, which resembled coins, were made of bronze, lead, ivory, bone, or terra-cotta.

How did such audiences behave? Professor Haigh offers this informative overview:

> The Athenians were a lively audience, and gave expression to their feelings in the most unmistakable manner. . . . The ordinary modes of signifying pleasure or disgust were much the same in ancient as in modern times, and consisted of hisses and groans on the one hand, and shouts and clapping of hands on the other. The Athenians had also a peculiar way of marking their disapproval of a performance by kicking with the heels of their sandals against the front of the stone benches on which they were sitting. Stones were occasionally thrown by an irate audience. . . . Country audiences . . . used figs and olives, and similar missiles, for pelting unpopular actors. . . . Certain types of character, which were generally to be met with among the [Athenian] audience, will easily be recognized as familiar figures. . . . There was the person who made himself objectionable to his neighbors by whistling an accompaniment to tunes which happened to please him. There were the "young men of the town," who took a malign pleasure in hissing a play off the stage. There were the people who brought out their [lunch or snacks] during the less exciting parts of the entertainment. There was the . . . individual who slept peacefully through tragedies and comedies, and was not even waked up by the noise of the audience going away.[10]

One major advantage Athenian audiences enjoyed over modern ones was the fact that at the time drama and theater were new institutions that existed nowhere else in the world. Theatrical conventions and ideas that today seem run-of-the-mill were, in fifth-century B.C. Athens, fresh and exciting. And it was in this stimulating, creative atmosphere that some of the greatest playwrights of all time worked their magic.

AESCHYLUS AND THE ESSENCE OF TRAGEDY

Of the four fifth-century B.C. master playwrights, three—Aeschylus, Sophocles, and Euripides—produced mainly tragedies. The essence of tragedy, as these writers developed it, was the struggle of human beings to reconcile the existence of both good and evil. The Greeks were the first people to recognize clearly the painful contradiction that ugliness and beauty inevitably coexist and that each, by sharp contrast, defines the other. And they came to realize that, to find and embrace the good, one must come to terms with the bad. Noted scholar and translator Paul Roche puts it this way:

> The theme of all tragedy is the sadness of life and the universality of evil. The inference the Greeks drew from this was *not* that life was not worth living, but that because it was worth living the obstacles to it were worth overcoming. Tragedy is the story of our existence trying to rear its head above the general shambles.[11]

Early playwrights like Thespis and Phrynichus had set the basic form and tone of tragedy. But it was not until the early fifth century B.C. that Aeschylus, the first major theatrical innovator after Thespis, raised the art of tragedy to the level of great literature. Born about 525, as a young man Aeschylus witnessed Athens's steady rise toward political, military, and cultural greatness. And one of the epic events connected with that rise became the major theme of his *Persians,* written circa 472. The oldest surviving complete tragedy, the play depicts with a compelling sense of immediacy the sweeping Greek victory over Persia in the naval battle of Salamis in 480.

Of the ninety plays Aeschylus reportedly wrote, eighty-two titles are known, but only seven complete manuscripts survive. Besides the *Persians,* these are *Seven Against Thebes* (written 467); the Oresteia, a trilogy consisting of *Agamemnon, The Libation Bearers,* and *The Eumenides* (458); *Sup-*

pliant Women (ca. 463); and *Prometheus Bound* (ca. 460). Aeschylus won his first victory in the City Dionysia contests in 484 and went on to win twelve more times.

One of Aeschylus's great innovations was the introduction of a second actor. Until his time, following the tradition established by Thespis, playwrights made do with one actor; but this limited them to telling fairly simple stories with a few characters, which the lone actor attempted to portray using different masks. The addition of a second actor significantly expanded the story-telling potential, since it allowed the depiction of twice as many characters.

Aeschylus also broadened the scope of drama by employing the trilogy, a series of three plays related in plot and theme. By allowing a story to unfold in three successive plays, he was able to show in much more detail the evolution and impact of a concept such as justice, greed, or fate. For example, the three plays of the Oresteia, the only Greek trilogy that has survived complete, trace a repeating pattern of revenge and murder in the generations of the family of Agamemnon, King of Argos. At the climax of the third play, the violent cycle is broken when the goddess Athena intervenes.

SOPHOCLES AND THE THIRD ACTOR

The second great fifth-century B.C. tragedian was Sophocles, Aeschylus's junior by some thirty years. Born around 496 at Colonus, then a village just outside Athens's city walls, Sophocles hailed from a well-to-do family and so received an excellent education. He grew up to play important roles in public affairs, for a time holding the office of treasurer of the large federation of city-states Athens headed in the mid-to-late fifth century. But such accomplishments were inevitably overshadowed by his reputation as the most successful dramatist ever to present plays in the Theater of Dionysus. In his first victory in the City Dionysia, in 468 (for a play titled *Triptolemus,* now lost), he defeated Aeschylus; and he went on to win first prize at least eighteen times. (According to ancient sources, he sometimes won the second prize, but never the third.)

In retrospect, Sophocles' impact on the theater, in his own time and for all times, was nothing less than extraordinary. To begin with, his output of plays was huge—reportedly 123 in all. Unfortunately, only seven of these have survived: *Ajax* (ca. 447), *Antigone* (ca. 441), *Oedipus the King* (ca. 429), *The*

Women of Trachis (ca. 428), *Electra* (ca. 415), *Philoctetes* (ca. 409), and *Oedipus at Colonus* (406).

Sophocles, a master of characterization, was the first playwright to use a third actor (and may also have employed a fourth toward the end of his career), which further increased the amount of character interaction in drama. The result of this development was a reduction in the importance of the chorus, the size of which he fixed at fifteen members. Sophocles' plots generally revolve around central characters whose personal flaws (often called "tragic" flaws) lead them to make mistakes that draw them and those around them into crises and suffering. During the climax of a Sophoclean tragedy, the main character recognizes his or her errors or crimes and accepts the punishment meted out by society and/or the gods.

The most famous example is the plight of the title character in *Oedipus the King.* Through the events of the story, Oedipus gradually learns that he has, unknowingly, killed his own father and married his own mother. Overwhelmed by the horror of these deeds, he accepts responsibility for them, blinds himself, and is doomed to wander the countryside as a moral leper.

EURIPIDES QUESTIONS TRADITIONAL VALUES

At the time that *Oedipus the King* first appeared before Athenian audiences, Euripides, the third giant of Greek tragedy, was already in his fifties and had competed often with Sophocles in the City Dionysia. Born in 485 B.C., the younger writer had his first plays produced in 455. Of a total of some 88, eighteen have survived, including *Alcestis* (438), *Medea* (431), *Heracles* (ca. 422), *The Trojan Women* (415), *Electra* (413), *Helen* (412), and *Iphigenia in Aulis* (ca. 405).

Euripides won the dramatic competitions only five times and was far less popular in his own day than either Aeschylus or Sophocles. This was primarily because Euripides' plays often questioned traditional and widely accepted social values. He suggested, for example, that life consists of a series of random events, so that the world operates more by chance than under the influence of the gods and preordained fate. In this view, human beings are just as concerned as the gods, or even more concerned, with establishing moral values.

In exploring how humans shape their own values and

destinies, Euripides also depicted ordinary people in highly realistic ways. Many Athenians saw this mode of expression as too undignified for the tragic stage, which they felt should show more heroic, larger-than-life people and themes. Thus, Euripides was far ahead of his time, and later scholars came to see him as the first playwright to deal with human problems in a modern way.

By focusing on the problems of real people, Euripides made the chorus even less important than Sophocles had. The real drama in Euripides' plays, comments Rex Warner,

> is confined to the men and women taking part in it. The chorus [members] perform in the role of sympathetic listeners and commentators, or . . . provide the audience with a kind of musical and poetic relief from the difficulties or horrors of the action.[12]

THE OLD COMEDY AND ARISTOPHANES

The final fifth-century B.C. theatrical great, Aristophanes, was a comic playwright. The exact origins of comedy are uncertain; but it is likely that it developed out of some of the same religious rituals that tragedy did. Most of the early Dionysian processions, including the dithyramb, were serious in nature. In time, however, some of these processions featured revelers dressed in animal costumes, particularly those depicting goats. These worshipers in their satyr outfits danced, sang, and exchanged off-color jokes with onlookers. That such processions were one important source of comedy is supported by the term's root words—*komos,* meaning "revel," and *aeidein,* meaning "to sing." Another source of Greek comedy appears to have been mimes, essentially improvised comic skits originally performed informally in town squares. When actors began writing these skits down, they were performed at theaters, becoming the precursors of full-fledged comic plays.

Although comedies first appeared on the program at the City Dionysia in 501, they did not receive official recognition, including government support for production and prizes, until 487. The winner of the first comedic contest was the playwright Chionides, of whom almost nothing is known. The most creative period for Greek comedy lasted from about 450 to 404 (often referred to as the Old Comedy, as opposed to the New Comedy, a less inventive version that thrived in the fourth and third centuries B.C.). The comic playwrights typically poked fun at people of all walks of life, but especially politicians, generals, and other leaders. "In no other place or age were men of all classes attacked and ridiculed in public and by name with such freedom" as in the Old Comedy, says noted scholar Victor Ehrenberg. "The ultimate reason for this . . . was the fact that comedy was an internal affair of the sovereign people as a whole, and so there was complete *parhesia*, freedom of speech."[13] Such freedom, James Butler adds, provided

> a license in language, situations, and stage portrayal difficult for us to realize fully, even today. It contained an incredible mixture of high [intellectual] and low [bawdy] comedy, satire, buffoonery, slapstick, verbal play, parody, allegory, metaphor, abuse, sex, caricature . . . singing, dancing, nudity, and vulgarity often in its crudest form.[14]

Aristophanes, who lived from about 445 to 388, was the undisputed master of the Old Comedy. Ancient writers attribute forty-four plays to him, but only eleven have survived, among the best known: *Clouds* (423), *Wasps* (422), *Peace* (421), *Birds* (414), *Lysistrata* (411), and *Frogs* (405). Throughout his career, Aristophanes used biting satire to poke fun at the leaders and institutions of his day, usually depicting them in fantastic or absurd situations. The heroes of *Birds*, for instance, attempt to build "Cuckoo City," a strife-free community in the sky. And in *Clouds*, a country gentleman visits the "Think-shop" of the philosopher Socrates, who sits in a basket suspended high in the air, there hoping to increase his chances of discovering the "secrets of the heavens." No matter how absurd, though, the parallels between such comic situations and the real ones they were meant to satirize were perfectly clear to Athenian audiences.

A MODEL FOR GREAT DRAMA

The theatrical reign of Aeschylus, Sophocles, Euripides, Aristophanes, and their contemporaries was short-lived. In 404 B.C., Athens went down to defeat in the conclusion of the horrific Peloponnesian War (which had engulfed all of Greece for twenty-seven years) and the golden age of Athenian culture more or less ended. The City Dionysia and its competitions among playwrights continued, to be sure. But the era of extraordinary innovation and enormous creative output was over.

The precise reasons that few, if any, more great Greek tragedies were written after the fifth century is unclear. Perhaps the playwrights felt that all that could be said in the tragic genre had already been said; or maybe audiences' tastes had changed in the wake of the great war's hardships and devastation. Likewise, the comedies of the post-war era were fewer, tamer, and less innovative and inspired. It is possible that the despair, depression, and disillusionment of the Athenians and other Greeks following the war dampened both the comic playwrights' creative zeal and audiences' appreciation for humor.

What is certain is that the plays of these masters continued to be performed in each succeeding generation. For indisputably, this handful of gifted individuals had, in a stroke, created the model for great drama and theater for all times.

NOTES

1. Rex Warner, trans., *Three Great Plays of Euripides*. New York: New American Library, 1958, p. viii.

2. Aristotle, *Poetics*, in Robert Maynard Hutchins, ed., *The Works of Aristotle*, in *Great Books of the Western World Series*. Chicago: Encyclopedia Britannica, 1952, p. 683.

3. This step was also revolutionary because it marked the first time that a non-priest had assumed the character of a god. It may have been quite controversial at the time, although no contemporary records from these festivals have survived to confirm it.

4. See Herodotus, *The Histories* 6.22, trans. Aubrey de Sélincourt, rev. A.R. Burn. New York: Penguin Books, 1972, p. 395. Because Athens had close ties with Miletus, most Athenians were distressed at their sister-city's fall. Herodotus goes on to say that the people fined Phrynichus a thousand drachmas (a huge sum at the time) for upsetting them and forbade anyone from re-staging the play.

5. James H. Butler, *The Theater and Drama of Greece and Rome*. San Francisco: Chandler Publishing, 1972, p. 6.

6. The Theatre of Dionysus survives in an advanced state of ruin. The best-preserved ancient Greek theater is the one at Epidauros (about 110 miles southwest of Athens), built circa 350 B.C. by the architect Polyclitus the Younger. It is 387 feet across and seats about 14,000. The Greek National Theatre and other modern theatrical groups periodically stage productions in it.

7. Bernard M.W. Knox, trans., *Oedipus the King*. New York: Pocket Books, 1959, pp. xxii–xxiii.

8. Over the years, playwrights tended to overuse the *machina* to show gods arriving in the finale to resolve the story's conflicts in a simple, neat way. Thus, the term *deus ex machina*, "the god from

the machine," eventually became a standard reference to any awkward, mechanical, or unconvincing means used by a playwright to resolve the plot.

9. Arthur E. Haigh, "The Attic Audience," in Lane Cooper, ed., *The Greek Genius and Its Influence.* Ithaca: Cornell University Press, 1952, p. 80.

10. Haigh, "The Attic Audience," pp. 80–81.

11. Paul Roche, trans., *The Orestes Plays of Aeschylus.* New York: New American Library, 1962, p. xvii.

12. Warner, *Three Great Plays of Euripides,* p. xviii.

13. Victor Ehrenberg, *The People of Aristophanes: A Sociology of Old Attic Comedy.* New York: Schocken Books, 1962, p. 26.

14. Butler, *The Theater and Drama of Greece and Rome,* p. 20.

The Nature of the Evidence

Greek
Drama

Surviving Records of Greek Drama

H.C. Baldry

How many of the plays of the golden age of Greek drama have survived the ravages of more than two millennia? And how much do we know about how these plays were originally staged? Former University of Southampton scholar H.C. Baldry answers these questions in the following discussion of the various ancient sources scholars draw on in their studies of ancient drama and theater. Baldry explains that the original play manuscripts likely underwent alterations over time and also points out that most of the surviving evidence, such as ruined theaters, descriptions by writers of later ages, and vase paintings and other artifacts (which he refers to as "monuments"), are often vague and unreliable.

[The first kind of evidence consists of the plays themselves.] It is easy to arrive at some conception of the number of plays produced in the fifth-century theatre at Athens. At every dramatic festival each of the three chosen tragic poets presented a trilogy—three tragedies which must have filled four hours or more of the day. A semi-comic play with a chorus of satyrs, also by the same author, followed as a short afterpiece. Comedy in its turn took the form of several single plays by different playwrights: the number varied at different periods. The total for all three types clearly adds up to hundreds; and the simplest and most sobering limitation on our knowledge and understanding of Greek drama is imposed by the fact that of all these hundreds of plays no more than a few dozen have survived. Fortunately for our purpose, the type best represented in our small collection is tragedy.

Out of all the tragedies originally performed in the fifth century B.C. we now possess thirty-two: seven by Aeschylus,

Excerpted from H.C. Baldry, *The Greek Tragic Theater* (New York: Norton). Copyright ©1971 by H.C. Baldry. Reprinted with permission of Chatto and Windus, London.

seven by Sophocles, eighteen attributed (one doubtfully) to Euripides. Some we can date with certainty: official festival records were kept, and parts of their information have reached us through one means or another—in inscriptions found on the slopes of the Acropolis or elsewhere, or in statements in our manuscripts of the plays. In some plays a topical allusion points to a likely year of first performance. Others again may be put in a conjectural order on grounds of style or treatment, though a recent discovery of a scrap of papyrus has shown that conclusions reached on these lines can be as much as thirty years wrong. The safest guide where other sources are lacking seems to be study of the playwright's changing metrical technique, which has already thrown a good deal of light on the chronology of the works of Euripides. The list we arrive at by these methods is as follows:

AESCHYLUS (525–456)

Persians	472	*Agamemnon*	458
Seven against Thebes	467	*Libation-Bearers*	458
Suppliant Women		*Eumenides*	458
Prometheus Bound			

The trilogy produced in 458 B.C. became known as the
    Oresteia.

SOPHOCLES (496–406)

Ajax		*Electra*	
Antigone		*Philoctetes*	409
Women of Trachis		*Oedipus at Colonus*	
King Oedipus			

EURIPIDES (458–406)

Alcestis	438	*The Madness of*	
Medea	431	*Heracles*	
Hippolytus	428	*Iphigenia among the*	
Children of Heracles		*Taurians*	
Andromache		*Helen*	412
Hecuba		*Ion*	
Suppliant Women		*Phoenician Women*	
Electra		*Orestes*	408
Trojan Women	415	*Iphigenia at Aulis*	
		Bacchae	

Attributed to Euripides: *Rhesus*

In addition to these complete texts many titles of lost tragedies are known, and thousands of 'fragments'—odd lines or parts of lines or brief passages, preserved on remnants of papyrus, or quoted for their moral sentiments or because they contain some unusual word or grammatical form. In some cases we can make a reasonable conjecture about the plot and characters of the play.

ALTERATIONS IN THE ORIGINAL TEXTS

How well does all this represent the words which the fifth-century audience heard spoken or sung in the theatre of Dionysus? There was no 'publication' of the play in the modern sense: the text which the author wrote had no law of copyright to protect it, and could easily be changed or varied when copies were made. Actors, in particular, were likely to delete lines or alter them or insert new passages of their own; and it is clear that our versions are not free from 'actors' interpolations'. The deviations were stopped, we are told, by the Athenian statesman Lycurgus, who about 330 B.C. introduced a law that an official copy of the tragedies of Aeschylus, Sophocles and Euripides should be kept and read over to the actors so that they could check their texts. This fourth-century authorised version may be the ultimate source from which our surviving plays come—a selection made largely for school use in Roman imperial times, though chance has added some others from an early complete edition of Euripides. The result is something very different from a random sample of fifth-century tragedy. Only the three outstanding playwrights are represented, and each of them by plays from his middle or old age: we have no complete work written by Aeschylus before he was fifty-four years old, or by Sophocles or Euripides before either was forty. Fortunately our collection includes some, at any rate, of those which were regarded as the best.

These plays were created primarily for performance, and must therefore have been performable: however strange some incidents or situations in them may seem to us, however baffling to a modern producer, they presumably contain nothing which could not be put before an audience within the limitations and conventions of the theatre of the time. But the texts themselves are uncertain guides to the way in which they were presented—how the words were spoken or sung, how actors or chorus moved, the scenery (if any) or the costumes. There are no stage directions, although it is possible that they once existed: a few, it is suspected, may have become incorporated in the spoken lines; others may be reproduced in marginal notes added at a later date ('he speaks angrily here', 'he must leap up'), but we cannot tell whether such a note reproduces an original direction or is merely an inference from the text. For the most part we are left with whatever conclusions we ourselves can draw from the poet's own words, and here we are faced with a crucial question. When the text describes a character's appearance or a scene, was the playwright referring to what was shown by material means in the theatre, or was he appealing to the audience's imagination, using verbal description all the more fully just because what he described was *not* visible to the eye? Given the text alone, there is no means of solving this puzzle except one's own preconceptions. . . . Although in a sense there can be no more reliable evidence for our purpose than the plays, the varied conclusions drawn from them by writers on the practical side of the Greek theatre show how difficult they are to use for that purpose and what treacherous guides they can be.

RUINED THEATRES

Second, the remains of ancient theatres; especially the theatre of Dionysus at the foot of the Acropolis in Athens, where the fifth-century tragedies were first presented. Here we can see the general shape and character of the original setting of drama; but when we look for more detail we are disappointed. The fifth-century structures in the theatre were mostly of wood, and few traces of them are left. What does survive is a complex collection of stone relics of various later stages in the theatre's history down to Roman imperial times.

Elsewhere in the Eastern Mediterranean there are many other Greek theatres dating from the fourth century B.C. or later. Some, like the outstanding example at Epidaurus, are much better preserved than their Athenian prototype and less overlaid with later changes and additions. To stand in the great Epidaurus theatre is an experience which in itself conveys some conception of Greek drama as it was originally performed. But again there is need for caution: in our search for information it is obviously dangerous to make inferences from these later sites for earlier practice at Athens. . . .

DESCRIPTIONS FROM LATER AGES

Third, ancient writers about drama and the theatre. In the modern world every aspect of theatre activity is described and discussed in print, but there was nothing of this kind in fifth-century Greece. The contemporaries of Sophocles and

Euripides were greatly interested in plays, but writers at any rate took the practical side of the theatre for granted and rarely mentioned it. The earliest full description of a Greek theatre that we possess comes from a Roman—the architect and military engineer Vitruvius. In the fifth book of his Latin work *On Architecture,* published late in the first century B.C., he distinguishes 'the Greek theatre' from its Roman counterpart and describes its lay-out precisely in geometrical terms—an ideal blueprint, not a portrayal of any particular example. Two centuries later still, a longer account is given by the Greek scholar Julius Pollux, together with passages dealing in some detail with costume and masks. These two authors of Roman times, centuries remote from Periclean Athens, provide most of our explicit literary information about the theatre and its use. Until the closing years of the last century their testimony was taken as evidence relevant to the fifth-century theatre, which was therefore endowed (for example) with a stage ten or twelve feet high. Today this is seen to be impossible. It is recognised that Vitruvius and Pollux draw largely on lost writers of the 'Hellenistic' period after Alexander the Great, so that much of what they say may be true of the second century B.C. and some of it may go back to still earlier practice; but they are no longer accepted as authorities for the time of the extant [surviving] tragedies. The same is true of various minor sources of a late date— short biographies of the playwrights, prefatory statements and marginal notes (known as 'scholia', by 'scholiasts') in our manuscripts of the plays, incidental comments by antiquarians and lexicographers. All these may contain some information that goes back to early origins, but how to sift the wheat from the chaff, the early from the late, is a puzzle to which there can be no sure solution.

The more we doubt this late evidence, the greater the need for scrutiny of writers closer in time to the great age of tragedy. They did not write explicitly about the theatre, but what can we read between the lines? What did they say in casual references, what did they imply or assume?

The most important contemporary source for many aspects of Greek tragedy is the surviving comedies of Aristophanes, dated between 425 and 388 B.C. One of the favourite subjects of his topical satire is the work of the tragic playwrights, especially Euripides. Anything he says or implies about the presentation of their plays is invaluable—

and sometimes what he does not say is equally significant.

When we turn to the fourth century, we are already moving away from the extant tragedies in time, and a question-mark hangs over any evidence we use. How far did the presentation of plays familiar to authors in this century differ from their staging in the fifth? It seems clear that the actor became more and more the centre of attention. and there was increasing emphasis on the musical side; but exactly what the differences were is an unanswerable problem. We can only be sure that the gap between fifth- and fourth-century theatre production was small when set against the contrast between both of them and the practices of Hellenistic and Roman times; nothing at all compared with the yawning abyss that separates them from theatre as we know it now.

Aristotle as a Witness

Consequently we must value any information we can glean from the fourth-century orators, or from the dialogues of Plato, who has much to say about tragedy in the *Republic* and the *Laws* and elsewhere; above all, from the principal fourth-century document concerned with drama, the *Poetics* of Aristotle, probably written soon after 335 B.C.

The importance of this brief and incomplete essay for the literary history of tragedy is obvious: to take only one point, Aristotle could read far more plays than we possess—probably all of Sophocles and Euripides and virtually all of Aeschylus, as well as many by other authors now lost. But one must not imagine him as merely an armchair reader of drama, sitting in the library of his philosophical school and toiling over his play-collection. For Aristotle, as one of his editors says, 'a tragedy is essentially something to be acted'. During his many years at Athens he must often have been present at the dramatic festivals, witnessing all those aspects of the performance—the spectacle, the setting, the music, the dance—of which we know so little. No one who reads his biological works can doubt that he would be a more observant theatre-goer than most. It is true that little of this background of experience emerges explicitly in the *Poetics*. Aristotle never describes the presentation of plays. What we get from him is (unfortunately) not description of theatrical practices, but tantalising reference and allusion: the rest is taken for granted as something familiar to all. But there is a point too often ignored . . . that underlying all he says about drama in the *Poetics* is a set of assumptions about its presentation; and if the picture we reconstruct from the rest of our evidence runs contrary to those assumptions, it is unlikely to be right.

PAINTINGS AND OTHER ARTIFACTS

Fourth, what are commonly called the 'monuments': vase-paintings, sculptures and statuettes, various other works of art which appear to depict some aspect of what was done in the theatre. Fresh discoveries in recent times have added to this mass of material until it now contains many hundred items. Its emergence has made scholars reconsider their attitude to the rest of the evidence, and has done more in this century than anything else to change our conception of Greek drama as it was originally performed.

Here again there are problems, some of which are not likely to be solved. Many items in the list can be given an approximate date and attributed to a definite source—sometimes, even to a named artist; but there are others which cannot, and until we know their date and where they came from their relevance to fifth-century Athens is hard to judge. Even when time and place of origin are known, the same question arises as over the literary evidence. How much can a picture drawn in 350 B.C. tell us about theatre production in the time of Sophocles? How far is a scene on a vase from the Greek communities in Southern Italy valid testimony for the use of the theatre at Athens? 'Monuments' of much later periods, like the writings of Vitruvius and Pollux, have now been largely discounted as evidence: we no longer think that a statuette of the second century A.D. is useful information about the tragic actor's costume six hundred years before. But for earlier work the point is more problematic, and the question of the time and distance gap has to be looked at afresh in every case.

There are other difficulties besides this, especially in dealing with vase-paintings. Often they portray a scene which might come from a play, but we cannot decide whether the figures in it are costumed actors or the characters of the story as the artist imagined them. In other instances connection with the theatre is certain: the figures wear or hold masks, or a flute-player is there to symbolise the fact that this is a play. But even here what we have before us is very different from a photograph. On the one hand, what the artist shows us is limited by the space available and the conventions of his technique. On the other, no realistic precision restricts his imagination: he may add to his picture human or divine beings who were not in the play, put into a theatre setting incidents which were narrated in a messenger's speech, turn the mask into an expressive face so that we see partly the actor, partly the character he represents. We must not treat as a factual record the artist's half-realised effort to express what was in his mind.

One last comment may be added as postscript to this brief and perhaps depressing survey. Where the handling of evidence of all types is so fraught with difficulty, it may well seem that the pursuit of truth is likely to be hopeless; and if each type were completely separate from the rest, this would be so. But conclusions can be reached by comparison across the field—by seeking out every link that can be found between the text of the plays, the other literary evidence, the remains of the theatre, and the 'monuments'.

CHAPTER 1

Characteristics and Conventions of Greek Drama

Greek
Drama

Home of Classic Drama: The Theater of Dionysus

James H. Butler

The Athenian Theater of Dionysus, in which the great fifth-century B.C. playwrights presented their works, became the model on which later Greek theaters were based. As University of Southern California scholar James H. Butler explains in this informative essay, Athens's renowned theater underwent numerous alterations and improvements over the years. Some of these occurred later in the Classic Age (ca. 500–323 B.C.) and others in the Hellenistic Age (ca. 323–31 B.C.) that followed.

The first theatre built in Greece was located in Athens. A number of authorities place the date for the erection of the earliest Theatre of Dionysus around 534 B.C., concurrent with the official start of tragedy. Some place it even earlier, about 550 B.C. The exact location of this theatre is also in dispute. One theory holds that the theatre was located in the agora, the ancient marketplace below the Acropolis. All that was required for these early performances was an open space for the performers, a *thymele* (an altar or sacrificial table), and temporary wooden *ikria* (bleachers) rising in tiers one above the other for seating the audience. It is reported in Suidas [a medieval Greek encyclopedia] that the bleachers collapsed and several people were killed during a contest in 499 B.C. among the dramatists Aeschylus, Pratinas, and Choerilus.

The following year the contest was moved to a sacred precinct on the south side of the Acropolis. An area dedicated to Dionysus was established around the middle of the sixth century B.C.; it contained a temple with a *thymele* in

Excerpted from James H. Butler, *The Theatre and Drama of Greece and Rome* (San Francisco: Chandler Publishing, 1972). Reprinted by permission of HarperCollins Publishers, Inc. (Endnotes in the original have been omitted in this reprint.)

front of it and an orchestra (dancing place) to accommodate early Dionysian ceremonies.

Another possibility suggested is that the first Athenian theatre was located from the beginning in the precinct of Dionysus and that it was there that the bleachers collapsed rather than in the agora.

CLASSICAL THEATRES

The Theatre of Dionysus which came into being in Athens in the fifth century B.C. following the bleacher incident assumed a position of tremendous importance. In this theatre the plays of Aeschylus, Sophocles, Euripides, Aristophanes, and the other prominent dramatists of the period were first performed. Moreover, this theatre was in use for centuries, changing its form and architectural details to conform to later developments. . . .

Something needs to be said about the general structural characteristics of classical Greek theatres. They eventually, with few exceptions, consisted of three distinct parts: *theatron* (viewing place) for spectators; orchestra (dancing place), where chorus and actors performed; and a later addition, a *skene* (scene building), which provided a scenic backing. The theatres were normally located near a populated area at the bottom of or cut out of a carefully selected, sloping hillside overlooking a seascape, a plain, or a city. If the chosen hillside consisted of suitable material (limestone), the theatre benches were simply carved out of it. This was true for the theatres at Argos (fourth century B.C.), Syracuse (fifth century B.C.), and Chaeronea (fourth century B.C.). The most common method was to bring in native stone for the seats. The circular orchestra located adjacent to and almost completely surrounded on three sides by the *theatron* was approximately 65 feet in diameter. On either side of the extremities of the *theatron* bordering the orchestra was open space for the *parodoi* (lateral entrances into the orchestra) used by chorus members for initial entrances into the playing area, by the actors suggesting in their stage appearance arrival from the harbor or distant parts, and by the audience to reach the lower sections of seats. In many theatres the *parodoi* developed subsequently into imposing stone gateways, like the ones at the Theatre of Epidauros. They helped to unify the separate parts of the theatre: *orchestra, skene,* and *theatron.* A *thymele* (altar) was usually located in the middle of the orchestra; however, it could be placed to one side of the orchestra, as it was in the Theatre of Thorikos and in the later Hellenistic Theatre of Priene.

The earliest scene buildings were very simple wooden structures. Later they were converted into increasingly complex stone buildings with *paraskenia* (side wings), several doors, a columned *proskenion* (section in front of the *skene*), an additional story, as well as other features. The development of the scene buildings into more complex structures paralleled the increased interest in acting, scenery, New Comedies rather than tragedies, and the diminished use of the chorus. In the Hellenistic theatres, the scene buildings with their raised stages dominated.

THEATRE OF DIONYSUS: EARLY ADDITIONS

The Theatre of Dionysus (ca. 499/8–ca. 150 B.C.) underwent at least four fundamental changes during the classical period and was not converted into a Hellenistic theatre until quite late, nearly 200 years after the latter made its appearance.

In the early part of the fifth century B.C., this theatre consisted of a circular orchestra area some 85 feet in diameter, cut out of the hillside, leveled, and hard-packed. It was supported on one side by a curved retaining wall, and in the center of the orchestra a *thymele* was placed. The theatre was located between the sloping south side of the Acropolis and the small Temple of Dionysus in the precinct of Dionysus. The *theatron* was the hillside, subsequently provided with wooden planks covering the earthen tiers dug out of the hillside. Presumably, there was no scene building. In this theatre were staged the earliest fifth-century Athenian dithyrambs, tragedies, Old Comedies, and satyr plays.

Exactly when the scene building first appeared in the Theatre of Dionysus is a question of uncertain answer. The first literary evidence of a scene building is found in *The Oresteia* of Aeschylus, produced in 458 B.C. One recent authority even dates the existence of some kind of a scene building in the earliest period. The early scene buildings were evidently quite crude, temporary wooden structures erected for each festival near the edge of the orchestra area and probably, because they occupied a portion of it, the orchestra was reduced in diameter from 85 to 65 feet. The scene buildings could serve as scenic backing for plays when needed and could also be used as dressing rooms for the actors.

When Pericles built his odeion (a roofed concert hall) in 446–442 B.C., immediately east of the Theatre of Dionysus, it encroached on the theatre. It thus became necessary to shift the orchestra and *theatron* a few feet to the northwest, thereby making the *theatron* steeper. The old curved retaining wall built to support the south side of the orchestra was replaced by a long straight wall consisting of large breccia blocks. Between this wall and the older Temple of Dionysus a long wooden hall, or stoa, about 200 feet long and 20 feet wide was constructed. The floor of the stoa was approximately 8 feet below the orchestra level, which was reached by a double flight of interior stairs. At the top of the stairs was a large opening in the north wall of the stoa about 23 feet wide leading out onto the orchestra terrace and onto a "T foundation" made of blocks of stone and flush with the orchestra level. It jutted out from the stoa opening about 10 feet and was about 25 feet wide. On either side of the "T foundation" located in the new retaining wall and independent of the stoa were 10 vertical stone grooves or slots which could be used to support temporary wooden scene buildings.

LATER ADDITIONS

The extensive changes made at the Theatre of Dionysus during the reign of Pericles also included the construction of a new, larger Temple of Dionysus south of the older one. [Noted scholar Arthur] Pickard-Cambridge gave this renovated Theatre of Dionysus the subtitle of "Periclean Theatre."

It is thought that the wooden stoa was replaced by one made of stone about 421–415 B.C.

The last major renovation of the Theatre of Dionysus in the classical period occurred during the term of the orator Lycurgus, who was in charge of Athenian finances from 338 to 326 B.C. This "Lycurgean Theatre" lasted until about 150 B.C., at which time it was converted into a Hellenistic theatre.

Lycurgus installed 78 rows of stone seats. These rested on a natural rock foundation and built-up earth. Divided into three sections separated by two passageways (*diazomata*), they seated from 14,000 to 17,000 people. The 67 special chair seats or thrones, each bearing the name of the priest or high official for whom it was reserved, were arranged in the first row facing the orchestra. Of these, 60 are still extant (dating perhaps from a later period). A special decorative throne, with holes near the feet for holding a supporting canopy for the priest of Dionysus, was located in the center of the row of chairs.

Between the orchestra and the stone stoa a new permanent stone *skene* was constructed with two projecting side wings (*paraskenia*) one or two stories high. This *skene* undoubtedly underwent several changes during the many years of its use. Perhaps stone columns were placed in front of it, or sections of it, such as the *paraskenia,* thereby creating a decorative *proskenion.* Excellent drainage facilities for the orchestra were completed and were much as they are today.

Scholars in the past few years have generally agreed that there was no raised stage in any of the classic theatres aside from small porches in front of the entrance to the *skene* or sets of steps leading from the orchestra into the *skene.* The raised stage was introduced into theatre building in Hellenistic times.

Greek Drama Was Based on Popular Myths

Michael Grant

Because ancient Greek drama evolved from religious
ritual, it was only natural that its principal themes
would be drawn from myths—the stories of the gods,
around whom such rituals revolved, and the humans
who had supposedly interacted with them in past
ages. Michael Grant, one of the twentieth-century's
most prolific and respected classical historians, here
explains how Attic (i.e., Athenian) drama incorporated the gods mentioned in the works of the early
poets Homer and Hesiod. He points out that, since
Greek audiences were already familiar with the stories of these gods, the playwrights did not need to
burden their texts with lengthy exposition (explana-
tory or background information). He then discusses
Aeschylus's trilogy, the *Oresteia*, as a prime example
of the use of myth in classic Greek drama.

In the "archaic" period of their culture, between the age of
epic and the Persian Wars (490–79), the distinctive literary
achievement of the Greeks had been, not yet tragic, but lyric
poetry. This was written both for singing and for recitation;
some odes were designed for solo performances, others—
with verse patterns attaining a high degree of complexity—
for chorus. Then, late in the sixth century at a fascinating
and explosive time of evolution for the city states, this sort of
poetry, in the hands of Simonides of Ceos and others, was
beginning to change its emphasis from personal topics to social, religious and moralizing themes.

From these beginnings came the genre by which myth
took on new life—Attic tragedy. How the development occurred has been endlessly and, in the lack of decisive evi-

Excerpted from Michael Grant, *Myths of the Greeks and Romans.* Copyright ©1962 by
Michael Grant. Reprinted by permission of the publisher, Weidenfeld and Nicolson,
London. (Endnotes in the original have been omitted in this reprint.)

dence, inconclusively discussed. But there appears to be a basis of truth in Aristotle's statement that tragedy evolved in the hands of those who led songs of rejoicing, accompanied by dances in honour of the god Dionysus. . . .

Although, with a few remarkable exceptions, Dionysus did not provide the themes of the plays, some of the earliest of them may have dealt with his story. But in any case the subject-matter of tragic drama was at all times closely related to religion. Indeed, the ecstatic [highly emotional, frenzied] . . . nature of the Dionysiac faith left its mark by the creation of an urgent, intense, religious spirit absent from our own drama. . . . It was the wine-like intoxicant of spiritual surrender which—to varying extents that we cannot now estimate—assisted the actors to interpret these plays, and the audiences to participate in their performance. They were more understanding audiences than any other western dramatists have known; for this was an epoch in which a small and gifted society, with slave-labour to support its shared traditions and culture, truly entered into the achievements of its great writers and artists.

MYTHS ILLUMINATED UNIVERSAL PROBLEMS

The subject-matter of the Athenian plays dealt with solemn fundamental matters concerning the relationship of mankind with the gods. That is to say, the subjects were mythological. The myths handed down from the Homeric and Hesiodic poems, as well as many more besides, had been retold by lyric poets writing in the intervening period. . . . And now remarkable further developments of this mythical material were on the way. The splendour of the dramatists' culture was far removed from saga, farther still from primitive memories (though these could still sometimes be detected in them): tragedy is unlike anything which developed from the myths of Polynesia or central Africa. Greek drama was a sophisticated symbol of profound, consciously appreciated issues, illuminating the universal problem through the individual case; just as the sculptors and vase-painters of this epoch, employing the same mythological themes, likewise attained new grandeur.

The Attic playwrights altered and transfigured the myths (as Shakespeare made use of Plutarch, the English chronicles, and the Italian romances), employing them as a traditional but elastic framework which gave the fullest scope for their originality. To Greek audiences these myths, although still capable of numerous variations (even at the hands of a single author), were familiar enough to enable much explanation to be saved. The tragedian could therefore concentrate on the essence of his task, which was the poetic, religious recreation of the past in the present. For the myths were the past to the Greeks, were real, and were therefore credible. Indeed distance aided contemplation, since although the first great tragedian Aeschylus was successful with his topical *Persae* [*The Persians*] about the battle of Salamis, his rival Phrynichus had earned condemnation for a tragedy about a painful contemporary happening, the capture of Miletus by the Persians. Universality was more easily attained by the treatment of myths instead, since they avoided any such concrete situation undetachable from topical events.

Yet, even in an age in which leading thinkers, with startling rapidity, were changing from mythopoeic to rational attitudes, mythology still gave expression to what engrossed or troubled people, and continued to provide the subject-matter for the great creative dramatists—rather as artists of the fourteenth century A.D. constantly repainted Biblical scenes and gained by doing so. Likewise, the Boeotian lyric poet Pindar of this same period (518–438 B.C.) interwove in almost all his odes—as an intimate part of his thought—some illuminating myth, in order to add surprise, universality and a moral (in tones either urgent or relaxed) to a topical occasion. . . .

DIALOGUE, CHORUS, AND MUSIC

The stages of tragedy's development from choral song are lost. We hear of a famous seventh-century lyre-player named Arion who was the first to compose songs, with a regular metre, in honour of Dionysus and to have them performed at Corinth; and at neighbouring Sicyon, the sixth century autocrat Clisthenes is said to have introduced choral singing in honour of the god. In the middle of that century an Attic box has a painting of a flutist playing to five skin-clad youths in tunics. Then, again in Attica, comes the name of the first known dramatist, Thespis. It may well have been he who converted "the answer to the chorus" into a regular actor impersonating a character; that is to say, responding to the chorus not in a choral metre but in the characteristic iambic verse-pattern of tragic narration, imitating the cadences of speech, which had evolved (notably in the hands of the statesman-sage Solon) in previous years. This extraneous element took the form of spoken dialogue or monologue interposed between the choral songs. And by thus representing and enacting a version of heroic myth, instead of merely singing about it, the new actor created drama and tragedy. Thespis came from Icaria (on Mount Pentelicon near Athens) where there was an old cult of Dionysus; and he introduced this novel variety of the choral art-form to Athens. There it was first given a public performance in c. 534 B.C., presumably with the support of Pisistratus who ruled the state. . . .

The historical development of tragedy explains what to us is one of the most unfamiliar features of this mythological drama, the prominent place it allows to the chorus and to choral odes. Alien to our own conventional realism, these odes were utilized (in different ways) by all the Attic tragedians; the choruses who pronounce them vary all the way from central figures in the play to peripheral observers. The chorus complements, illustrates, universalizes, or dramatically justifies the course of events; it comments or moralizes or mythologizes upon what happens, and opens up the spiritual dimension of the theme or displays the reaction of public opinion. . . . So the twelve, or later fifteen, singers and dancers of the chorus played a vital part in the perpetuation and transfiguration of the myths which was tragedy's achievement.

Yet we cannot assess this role of the chorus fully, since we cannot reconstruct the musical accompaniment which was its integral constituent and which the Greeks regarded as their greatest art, inseparable from poetry and essential to the harmony of speech, song and dance which made tragedy what it was. Less than twenty more or less fragmentary scores have survived, and of these the only unmistakable setting of a tragedy is the tattered score of a few lines of Euripides. If more of this music had survived, the tragic treatment of mythology would assume a vital new dimension for us; though I doubt if this would make the plays more readily accessible to our minds, since alien music comes hard to western ears, as travellers to Asia know. Since the Renaissance, however, composers of operas on mythological themes have been free to display, according to their own talents, their recognition of the all-important role which music must have played in the original productions.

A FEROCITY OF THOUGHT AND MEANING

The titles of 525 Greek tragedies are known (at least a quarter of the titles, relating to familiar mythical themes, are used again and again), and of these only 34 plays are preserved complete or almost complete. Although we know the names of many playwrights, the surviving tragedies are by Aeschylus, Sophocles and Euripides. Their plays are short by our standards—shorter than two acts of *Hamlet*—but in the semi-circular theatres audiences of 10,000 and more sat watching and listening for seven or eight hours a day. The scene, usually simple, was rarely changed (twice, exceptionally, in Aeschylus' *Eumenides*), and the chorus seldom left the stage. The actors, men or boys (apart from mutes), gradually rose to three in number, with a fourth very rarely—only for a brief scene or two at the end of the fifth century: the doubling of nine to eleven parts in Euripides must have been a strain. Costumes and masks were conventional, stressing the religious awe felt for the strange world that was being enacted; and when Euripides attempted greater realism, he was criticized.

Poetry depicts the larger passions, and the permanent and universal themes enshrined in the myths, more effectively than prose. Indeed all the world's greatest plays, mythological or otherwise, have been in poetic language. Poetry rises beyond the limitations of the theatrical framework, and gives drama the opportunity to understand and present the great issues of life in a dimension which neither science nor theology can attain. The methods of the theatre are at once subtle and direct, and in the Greek open-air stage and the long daily sessions they had to be raised to the highest degree of dramatic vividness. Thus in Attic tragedy, although certain unfamiliar conventions such as the chorus seem to us to hold up the action, and although incident and movement are sometimes scarce in comparison with the physical activity of an Elizabethan or modern play, there was an immense economy and a concentrated, irremediably speeding ferocity of thought and meaning. The myths made this possible. Much of the action, as the audience knew, had already happened before the play began. This . . . directed their eyes upon the sharply explicit foreground in which fundamental problems were presented in the most vigorous and concrete form.

AESCHYLUS'S USE OF MYTHS

Out of the ninety plays attributed to Aeschylus, and performed from c. 499–6 B.C. until his death in 456, seven have
come down to us. We have not enough secure dates to draw
any useful conclusions about the chronological development of his art; but his most important technical innovation
was the introduction of a second actor, which created the
possibility of a dramatic situation or conflict. Aeschylus is
also responsible for a new seriousness, a lofty intellectual
tone conveyed through a densely charged style of massive
grandeur and stiffly gorgeous, exuberant complexity. For
[English poet] Robert Browning, as for others,

> Aeschylus' bronze-throat eagle-bark at blood
> Has somehow spoilt my taste for twitterings.

In veiled, oracular speech, loaded with a multiplicity of dar-
ing, inventive words and symbols, he mobilized his imaginative power to write into the myths almost incommunica-
ble cosmic and human truths.

One of the most famous of the mythological cycles elabo-
rated by the tragedies relates to the gory tale of the House of
Pelops and Atreus. These stories were located at Argos by
Aeschylus, as earlier (in the *Odyssey*) at its neighbour and
forerunner Mycenae. Perhaps the . . . tradition echoes a real
Mycenaean ruling house, whose alleged foreign origin may
reflect early immigration from Asia Minor. After grim pre-
liminaries in previous generations, the story comprises six
crimes: the seduction by Thyestes of Aerope, the wife of his
brother Atreus; the murder by Atreus of Thyestes' children
(whose remains were set before their own father to eat); the
abduction to Troy, by Paris, of Helen the wife of Atreus'
younger son Menelaus; the sacrifice by Agamemnon (Menelaus' brother) of his own daughter Iphigenia; the murder of
Agamemnon, on his return from Troy, by his wife Clytemnestra and her lover Aegisthus . . . and the murders of Clytemnestra and Aegisthus by her offspring Orestes and Electra.

The plays in Agamemnon's trilogy known as the *Oresteia*
deal successively, as has been seen, with the death of
Agamemnon, the deaths of Clytemnestra and Aegisthus, and
the termination of the blood-feud by divine intervention.
This is the only surviving trilogy of any tragedian; it may
have been accompanied by a satyr-play about the wanderings of Menelaus.

Parts of the story must be very ancient—the sacrifice of Iphigenia, for example, no doubt goes back to times of human sacrifice. The *Odyssey* had held up the fate of Agamemnon as a warning and contrast to the destiny of Odysseus, and hinted at the murder of Clytemnestra by Orestes. But the paucity of references to this story in the two principal Homeric poems shows that Aeschylus was too modest if he described his subjects as "slices from the great banquet of Homer." The tragic implications of Agamemnon's story are far from Homeric, reflecting rather the religion and morality of the guilt-culture which followed and largely superseded the shame-culture of *Iliad* and *Odyssey.*

From the later seventh century B.C. onwards, the theme inspired artists; sculptural reliefs from the sixth-century Treasury of the Heraeum on the river Silerus (Foce da Sele) in south-west Italy show Orestes killing Aegisthus, and Clytemnestra forcibly restrained—perhaps by Orestes' nurse—from attacking her son. The lyric poet Stesichorus (though transferring the scene to Sparta) introduced much of the material subsequently used by Aeschylus. . . . The subject-matter of such myths seemed to [English writer] H.G. Wells, in *The New Machiavelli*, "the telling of incomprehensible parricides . . . of gods faded beyond symbolism, of that Relentless Law we did believe in for a moment, that no modern western European can believe in." Nevertheless, the *Oresteia* displays one of the world's outstanding arts in all its glory, presented to a vital, responsive community by an idiosyncratic genius of inexhaustible poetic versatility and strength. [English poet Algernon] Swinburne described the plays as "probably on the whole the greatest spiritual work of man."

How Sophocles Used the Chorus

G.M. Kirkwood

Of all the theatrical devices used by the ancient Greek dramatists, the chorus perhaps seems the strangest to modern audiences. Standing on-stage during the entire play, the chorus periodically breaks into poetic songs, variously known as odes, *stasima* (singular is *stasimon*), and *parodoi* (singular is *parodos*). Often, the Greek chorus is too easily explained away simply as a group of observers who "comment" on the action of the story. The chorus does comment, of course, but it also can and does perform a multitude of other functions, depending on the situation and the inventiveness of the playwright. In this essay, former Cornell University professor G.M. Kirkwood focuses primarily on the highly varied and inventive use of the chorus by Sophocles, the middle man in the triad of great fifth-century B.C. tragedians.

What part does the chorus play in Sophoclean drama? Most conspicuously, it sings lyrical songs. Many of the songs are of remarkable poetic grace, and some express deeply felt religious and moral ideas with great power and beauty. The lyrics of tragedy are, along with [the ancient Greek poet] Pindar, our main possession of Greek choral poetry.

Some of these songs can be read satisfactorily when detached from their context. The famous ode on man which is the first stasimon [choral song] of *Antigone*, the second stasimon of *Oedipus Tyrannus* with its prayer that the singers may live in piety under the law of heaven, the ode in praise of Colonus and Attica in *Oedipus at Colonus*, and the song in *Antigone* on Danae, Lycurgus, and Cleopatra are self-sufficient lyric poems, complete and enjoyable in themselves. If they had been transmitted to us alone, we could barely determine that they belonged in plays, and we could

Reprinted from G.M. Kirkwood, *A Study of Sophoclean Drama.* Copyright ©1958 Cornell University. Used by permission of the publisher, Cornell University Press.

not possibly say from what kind of dramatic context they had been lifted. Other odes, while more extensively linked to the context [of plays], are still independent enough in content to be thoroughly intelligible alone: in *Ajax* the ode addressed to Salamis and that on the sorrows of war, Stasimon Two of *Antigone* on the troubles of the house of Labdacus, and the ode on old age in *OC* [*Oedipus at Colonus*]. Even in odes that are so closely woven into their context that they form a commentary on the immediate action, Sophocles has a way of starting with a general idea or a thought removed from the immediate matter and only later circling back to the situation of the play. . . .

The detachment that marks so many of Sophocles' choral songs raises problems when we think about the meaning of the odes in relation to the plays. If all the lyrics were as immediately and obviously concerned with the action as, for example, Stasimon Three of *The Trachinian Women*, in which the chorus reveal their recognition of what the oracle given to Heracles really meant and describe what Heracles has suffered and Deianeira done, we should have no serious trouble in assigning the lyrics their place in the action. Such an ode obviously has the simple function of providing a lyrical commentary on the events of the play. By the poetic intensity and grace of its diction and rhythm it adds a further dimension of meaning and dramatic force to those events. But immediacy and simplicity of reference are found in less than half the odes. There are also general reflections on the nature of man, on piety, on old age, on the beauties of Attica, on the power of love. What are we to make of these?

One way to dispose of [explain] them is to treat them simply as independent lyrics expressing Sophocles' thoughts about the various matters on which they touch. If they seem totally irrelevant, then never mind the context; their own beauty and profundity are enough to justify their presence, and convention demanded that the action of the play be broken by lyrical passages. This somewhat cavalier [casual] procedure is followed by some critics and probably many readers; we often see choral passages quoted, without context or reference to context, as examples of what Sophocles thought. . . .

THE CHORUS AS ONE OF THE ACTORS

There is another way of approach to the choral odes, an approach by which they are neither studied in a vacuum nor assumed to be Sophocles' sentiments. It is possible to assume that the odes spring from the mind of the chorus, as a character or, to be more exact, a group of undifferentiated characters of the drama in a precise set of circumstances, and to see what connection they have with the action that forms their context. The context need not be only the episodes immediately preceding and following. It may involve the structure and rhythm of the play as a whole, the personality of the chorus, their relation to the other persons of the drama. . . .

There are good reasons for using this approach. In the first place, there are some odes that quite obviously do not represent what Sophocles thought about the situation in hand but only what the group of persons forming the chorus thought, without suggesting either profundity [great insight] or vacuity [ignorance] in their thought. In Stasimon Two of *Ajax* the chorus joyfully and mistakenly think that Ajax will not commit suicide. The fact that the chorus are mistaken in their joy does not destroy the force of the song (in fact it helps to create its dramatic force), because it is not a mistaken moral judgment . . . but a mistaken view of events. Secondly, Sophoclean choral odes are quite conspicuously suited to the group of singers. Just those choral songs that seem most detached in content are sung by choruses that are most detached, grave, and self-reliant. The choral ode on old age is sung by old men; the ode in praise of Attica by Atticans. Nowhere in Sophocles' plays is there a contradiction in the attitude of the chorus between its songs and its other utterances. This adaptation of the content of choral songs to the attitude and personality of the singers does not arise by accident.

We have external evidence both from a highly reputable critic who undoubtedly knew more of Sophocles' plays than we do and from Sophocles himself that suggests that this approach is valid: in praising the Sophoclean chorus Aristotle clearly implies that it has its place in the drama as "one of the actors.". . . There is [also] Sophocles' capacity for remaining inside the myth and never stepping outside it to explain or to reveal to us his point of view about what is happening. If we look for the sentiments of the poet in Sophoclean odes, we are in search of what is unlikely to be presented explicitly by a playwright whose whole way of procedure is not to criticize and reshape but to work within the myth. . . .

There are two distinct types of personal relationship be-

tween the choral group and the action and persons around them. The choruses of *Ajax*, *The Trachinian Women*, *Electra*, and *Philoctetes* are closely attached each to one character: to Ajax, Deianeira, Electra, and Neoptolemus, respectively. In these four plays the choruses are by no means impartial; their sympathies . . . are with a single person, and they share his point of view. They do not echo every word of their champion, for they are not merely extensions of his personality; they have their own nature and some independence of thought. The sailors in *Ajax* warn their leader against undue boastfulness, and those in *Philoctetes* express their sympathy for Philoctetes before Neoptolemus has begun to feel any. But in the larger issues they stand firm with their favorite's prejudices and interests as they see them: Ajax's men are as mistakenly bitter toward Odysseus as Ajax is. . . .

In the other three plays the choruses are more independent. In *Antigone* and *Oedipus at Colonus* it is clear that, wherever their sympathies may lie, the choruses are primarily elders of Thebes and Colonus, respectively, and their attitude to what is going on is always shaped by the responsibilities and special interests of their position. In *Oedipus Tyrannus* they are devoted to Oedipus; but in the very passage in which they most firmly state their devotion, it is quite clear that they feel a civic rather than a strictly personal loyalty (unlike the chorus of *Ajax*); it is Oedipus as savior of Thebes whom they revere: "For the winged maiden came upon him, a manifest thing, and in the test he was proved wise and a blessing to the city; therefore he shall never be judged guilty of evil by my judgment.". . .

DEPENDENT AND INDEPENDENT CHORUSES

We are now ready to look at the choral songs, the parodoi and stasima, sung by the chorus alone. We shall find that the distinction between two choral relationships to the drama . . . is only a preliminary issue here and will only help a little toward clarifying this part of the chorus's role. Even in choral odes where we can clearly detect an air of independent judgment there is much more to be taken into account. But a beginning can be made with this point. We have noticed that those odes that have, beyond others, an air of detachment are sung by choruses whose measure of independence as persons is greatest: Stasimon One of *Antigone*, Stasimon Two of *Oedipus Tyrannus*, Stasimon One of *Oedipus at Colonus*. Is

there a corresponding immediacy and dependence in odes sung by choruses who are personally dependent? . . .

In *Ajax*, from the opening words "Telamonian Ajax," throughout the song, the chorus express their concern, devotion, and dependence. In *The Trachinian Women* the burden of the parodos is Heracles: Where is he? May he come! Zeus will protect him. But the chorus are thinking about Heracles from Deianeira's point of view; they are grieved by her grief and concern for him, and they urge her to be confident. There is not, certainly, dependence as in *Ajax*, but there is intense personal sympathy. In *Antigone* and *Oedipus Tyrannus* there is concern also, but concern for the city of Thebes. In *Antigone* the theme of the ode is joy and pride at the victory of Thebes over the Seven, with a counterpoint of sorrow for the death of the two sons of Oedipus. In *OT* [*Oedipus Tyrannus*] the ode is a cry of distress at the plight of Thebes and a prayer to the gods to help Thebes against the ravages of plague.

Once again, then, we find the familiar distinction between personal and impersonal, attached and independent choruses. To pursue our analysis throughout the odes would be tedious and unnecessary; we should find that the same relation between the personality of the choral group and the nature of its songs is steadily maintained. . . .

HOW SOPHOCLES' CHORUSES DIFFERED FROM THOSE OF HIS RIVALS

To see that this careful and consistent relating of choral songs to choral personality is distinctively Sophoclean, it will be useful to look for a moment at some aspects of the choral manner of Aeschylus and Euripides. The choruses of Aeschylus are certainly dramatic, though not all of them in the same way. One type is most strikingly exemplified by *The Suppliants*, where the choral group is, of course, the protagonist. . . . A different kind of dramatic chorus appears in *The Persians* and, with more imposing grandeur, in *Agamemnon*; here the episodes are, broadly speaking, illustrations of the theme, which finds its fullest expression and is made universal in the choral odes. Euripides sometimes uses the chorus in this second Aeschylean manner. In *The Trojan Women* . . . the lyrics are the shaping and unifying element of the play. . . .

It never has been suggested, so far as I know, that any

chorus of Sophocles is the protagonist; but it has often been supposed that his choruses convey the dramatic theme, more or less in the manner of *Agamemnon*. . . .

Euripides clearly did not have the same interest as Sophocles in preserving the "character" of the chorus in the sense of carefully adapting the thought and manner of the songs to the personality and situation of the choral group. Nor is this difference just a matter of choral personality; it tells us something about the difference in attitude between Sophocles and Euripides toward dramatic structure. In the choral odes as elsewhere Euripides is the more detached and abstract playwright; with Sophocles everything is personal and immediate. It does not at all follow that Euripidean dramatic form is inferior, only that it is different and that it does not have the same kind of unbroken tension that is the hallmark of Sophoclean form.

USING THE CHORUS TO MOVE THE PLOT ALONG

In this comparison of Sophoclean and Euripidean manner we are . . . dealing with a question of structure as well as choral personality. We must now, in order to complete our account of Sophocles' disposal of his chorus, look at several further aspects of it that bear more essentially on structure than on character drawing. . . .

In the parodos of *Antigone* the chorus tell of the defeat of the Argive army and the triumph of Thebes. Immediately after it Creon enters and makes his specious inaugural address. In *Antigone* . . . the prologue and the first episode introduce two different elements of the theme. The parodos is accommodated to this structure; the Theban elders know nothing of Antigone's anger or her determination to flout the edict of the new monarch, and their song of victory is in complete contrast to the passion and excitement of the prologue. Its connection with the following scene is just the reverse of this relationship of contrast. With its dominant theme of victory it provides exactly the right tone for the introduction of the scene. It also, of course, gives information about the repulse of the invading army, but what is dramatically important is its spirit, which blends perfectly with the proud and confident tone of Creon's opening address and thus contributes to the ultimate irony of the contrast between this lofty beginning and the tumultuous and undignified incident after the guard's arrival. Thus the tone of the

ode, by its contrast with what goes before and its adaptation to the mood that follows, is structurally valuable.

The parodos of *Oedipus Tyrannus* adapts the same principle to different circumstances. In the prologue Creon returns from Delphi to announce that the plague will end only if the murderer of Laius is driven from Thebes. The first episode begins with Oedipus' proclamation to the people, commanding them to reveal the murderer if they can. There is no contrast, in the spirit or content, between the two scenes; *Oedipus* is a play of continuous dramatic development. There might therefore seem to be no dramatic use for the parodos beyond linking prologue to episode by lyrical repetition of key ideas in the prologue. . . . Certainly the parodos does perform this service, but it also does more, and its additional role is typically Sophoclean. The song has three themes: inquiry about the meaning of the oracle, lament for the ravages of the plague, and prayer invoking the aid of Athena, Artemis, Apollo, Zeus, and Dionysus. All three are continuations of themes begun in the prologue, but that of prayer, which is dominant in the ode, has an additional force. . . .

A Song to Relieve the Tension

There is one more kind of structural effect achieved by Sophoclean choral odes that deserves mention, although it is essentially a negative effect: while the odes we have been noticing have, by contrast or suspense or ambiguity, created or enhanced dramatic tension, these odes to some degree relax the intensity of a situation. Perhaps they are no more than instances of songs in the "classical style," but two of them in particular, *Oedipus Tyrannus* and *Antigone*, have so pronounced an effect on the rhythm of the dramatic action that they require separate mention.

The *Oedipus* ode begins with an agonized lament for the fate of mankind:

> Woe for the generations of man! Your lives are equal to nothingness in my reckoning. What man ever has more of prosperity than its mere seeming, and after the seeming, a decline?

Then, in a lyrical review of Oedipus' greatness and suffering, the chorus give voice to the emotional stress that has been built up almost beyond endurance in the terrible incident that precedes, and by giving voice to it they bring a measure of relief. Gloomy and despairing though their cry is, it yet calms and brings a lull in the action. . . . Structurally

the function of the ode is modest, but its fine emotional consummation of the catastrophe makes it at once lyrically great and dramatically appropriate.

In *Antigone* the corresponding ode is sung just after Antigone has been led off to be imprisoned. It tells of three imprisonments: of Danae, Lycurgus, and Cleopatra. It is a striking poem.... Here, as generally, the contribution of the ode is very simple: instead of moral pronouncement we have a poetic elaboration, very moving and vivid, of the single theme of imprisonment, forming a kind of lyrical finale to the foregoing scene. It is the emotion of the chorus, and the imaginative reach of their song, not their intellectual prowess, that count here.... The ode is a transformation of the pathos of events into lyrical terms that fulfill and give respite from the tragic action. Then the plot is renewed with the Teiresias scene.

USING THE CHORUS TO PREACH?

Finally, something should be said about the second stasimon of *Oedipus Tyrannus.* Of its two lyrical systems, the first contains a prayer for piety and reverence and a condemnation of *hybris* [arrogance]; the second expresses the hope that evil practices may be punished and ends with the fervent wish that Apollo's oracles may be fulfilled and the fear that religion is vanishing from the earth. Because of its devoutly religious tone the ode creates a very strong impression. It is frequently made to bear an interpretative weight in relation to the play as a whole that it does not deserve. To one critic this is one of just two passages "where we feel certain that Sophocles is preaching." But if Sophocles is preaching here, what is the point of the sermon in relation to the play? Does it charge Oedipus with *hybris*? ... It is extremely difficult to find confirmation in the rest of the play for this judgment, and therefore we may well hesitate to regard it as such....

What, then, are the dramatic qualities of the ode? First, it is relevant to the context—not just because it discusses topics that have a place in the episodes before and after, but also, and mainly, because the manner in which the chorus make their reflections is fitting both to the personality of the elders and to the dramatic atmosphere in which the ode is set. Secondly, instead of interrupting the course of the drama with a sermon by Sophocles, settling moral and religious problems, the words of this ode simply express, in language of vigor and beauty, the religious thoughts of the chorus, evoked by their doubts and anxiety. The ode settles nothing. But as in the *Antigone* odes the very ambiguity and inconclusiveness of the song increase dramatic tension, where a sermon would break it. Finally, there is a distinctively Sophoclean touch in the ironical interplay between the ode, Jocasta's prayer, and the appearance of the Corinthian.

The above sketch of how the chorus fits into Sophoclean drama is frankly incomplete. An attempt to give an exhaustive account would necessitate discussion of imagery and meter and study of the thought of the odes at some length. ... We have seen that, consistently and effectively, Sophocles keeps the spirit and the thought of his choral songs in line with the personality and the immediate position and attitude of the group of singers. And we have seen also that he often goes beyond this kind of dramatic relevance to create various effects of contrast, suspense, relief, irony, and ambiguity, which contribute to the effectiveness of the action.... The choral group is a character, and its personality and its relation to other characters are worked out with the same skill that Sophocles expends on the rest of his character portrayal; and the choral songs are integral parts of the dramatic structure, contributing, like the other parts, to the compact shape and the subtle rhythm of the whole.

Masks Highlighted the Characters

Iris Brooke

It has long been common knowledge that fifth-century B.C. Greek actors wore masks when performing. But the materials used to make these masks, as well as their exact appearance and the specific characters they represented, are not so well understood (although there were surely masks for standard characters such as kings, young men, old women, and the half-man-half-goat satyrs). As scholar Iris Brooke, formerly of the Department of Classics at Bristol University, points out here, this is partly because no masks from Greece's Classic Age have survived. Also, she explains, most of the ancient references to the use of theatrical masks are from later Greek and Roman times, written when the appearance of the masks had changed considerably.

The fascinating study of masks has probably caused more headaches and misunderstandings than any other in the history of classic theatre. The chief difficulty is that there is very little evidence available concerning the masks worn for the early tragedies and comedies; yet there is a vast amount of information to be found during the late Hellenistic and Roman periods. This is a quite natural but infuriating state of affairs. We are interested primarily in the lifetime of the great dramatists, a comparatively short period of a hundred years—whereas the period that came after, which is still sometimes referred to as classic, lasted roughly six hundred years. There is, therefore, considerably more information to be had about the masks that were used by actors from the Hellenistic times (late fourth century B.C. onwards), and these were quite obviously stylized versions of the original. Examples of fifth-century masks clearly show us that they were not exaggerated but representational.

It appears that during the late fourth century there was a general tendency to create an exaggerated kind of mask, both for tragedy and comedy. This emphasized and enlarged the features in every way so that the mouth was made much bigger than life and always appeared wide open, expressive of agony or laughter as the case might be; the eyes were made larger or smaller than normal and the hair built up in the front of the head to form a crest or crown. In most instances the whole mask was much bigger than life. This form of hair-dressing or building-up (*onkos*) is peculiar to the masks only from the fourth century onwards; by the beginning of the third century this particular feature had become an established and recognized feature of theatre costume.

CLARIFYING MISUNDERSTANDINGS

The sources of our written information on the theatre come from the hands of Roman scholars. It is therefore not at all surprising to find that what was to them a traditional and well-established formula governing the playing of the old tragedies and comedies was accepted without further question as the original classic method of presentation. The Romans were hardly in a position to do any extensive research into the styles of four centuries earlier; it is only of comparatively recent years, when both travel to the ancient sites and photography have made research so much easier, that a grain of doubt was sown in the minds of scholars, especially when more extensive study of fragments of pottery disclosed the fact that during the fifth and fourth centuries B.C. such masks as were illustrated did not entirely conform to the descriptions given by Julius Pollux [a second-century A.D. Greek scholar]. This, then, is one of the misunderstandings which I hope is clarified. There is yet another which is almost as troublesome and arises from the primitive use of masks, that of disguise or identification. Tradition makes the classic mask an invention of Thespis who was supposed to have given the first performance of tragedy; in order to do so with realism he chose to disguise his face. In the first stages, we are told, this was done with a make-up of some sort, but gradually the idea of a mask to obliterate expression was carried into practice and a plain linen mask was invented. This story completely ignores or by-passes one of the primitive uses of masks—that of striking terror or awe into the hearts of any audience by the presentation of an inhuman and static head on a body that is human and moves. Masks have been used for this purpose since the beginning of human consciousness, and to this day they are still used expressly for this purpose by certain peoples. Witch-doctors and mystic dancers alike all over the world have found this sort of disguise or identification of supreme use to endow their movements with a sense of unearthliness. A mask can hold an audience spellbound, shocked or mesmerized; such qualities could not have been unknown to any actor at any time. Even the Corinthian helmet with its frightening face-piece was invented before Thespis.

Curiously enough the comic mask as it has come down to us is not a laughable thing unless one is prepared for it. However funny the expression may be, the same inhuman quality exists and any small child will be frightened by its first vision of anything so like and unlike reality. So the story of Thespis' mask would seem to be as out of date as many other theories that surround the theatre of ancient Greece. Perhaps it was a mask of linen that Thespis invented, something modelled and shaped into a firm structure that looked more lifelike than those of wood or other less plastic materials. It could not have been the first mask. The introduction of a tragic mask, coloured and modelled with impressive grandeur, is attributed to Aeschylus.

MATERIALS AND USES

There remains no definite evidence as to the exact details of such masks, for naturally there is none in existence. The very fact that they originally had to be light enough in weight to be worn by any actor in reasonable comfort rules out any possibility of their survival. We are not aware of their actual construction, although various artists illustrated them from different angles and do show us some quite valuable and interesting points. We can see, for instance, that the hair was all part of the mask and not a separate wig. Such hair could have been human hair arranged in a suitable manner and set after the fashions of the day. It could, on the other hand, have been made from some animal hair or some such substance as tow. Certainly in the later masks of the Hellenistic and Roman theatre, the hair is so stylized that it has very little similarity to human hair. The coarseness and over-exaggeration of the features required some treatment that was much larger than life. The mask itself was made from carved wood, cork or leather, or perhaps it was stiffened linen, moulded on a marble face in much the same manner as a papier-mâché one can be today. This idea is one that appeals to me, because, if this were the case, it might account a little for the vast number of mask heads that still exist. However, it would only account for a very limited number of such heads, for the majority of them are either much too large or much too small to have been used for this purpose. It remains an interesting thought.

What colours were used to establish the identity of different types of persons we have no idea, for it is useless to attach any importance to Pollux's views on the original tragic masks. His writings tell us specifically of the character masks existing in his own day, not of the tragic masks that could be identified with the works of Aeschylus. Some of them could perhaps be acceptable as a guide to the more general types that appear in Euripides' and Aristophanes' plays. Anyway we do know that masks were worn from the time of Aeschylus' tragedies, their purpose being primarily to identify the actor to his audience when he was playing two or more parts and had to make speedy and obvious changes of character. They were also worn by the chorus to give unity and credibility to a group of young men who were taking the parts of the chorus, which might be representing a variety of types, both male and female, old and young, foreigners and sailors, and even animals and birds. From the pictures that have come down to us it would seem that a chorus, more often than not, wore identical masks. They were almost always intended to represent a community without any individuality. Obviously the best method of fulfilling their purpose was for them to wear identical masks, though there does not seem to be any proof that costumes needed to be identical. So here again is a perfectly good *raison d'être* [rationale] for the importance of the mask. We must remember that the vast open-air theatres, with their seating capacities for 17,000 and 14,000, would really need a clearly defined head with a simple formality about it that could be easily distinguished in the distance. The variety of colouring and features that occur normally in any collection of individuals could be best overcome by the use of masks.

We may assume that the early masks used by Aeschylus were neither exaggerated in expression nor size. Their colouring might, however, have been in some way distinguishing; whiter skin tone for women perhaps in normal choruses, though we do know that in the *Suppliants* of Aeschylus there is a reference to these young women being dark-skinned. Probably the *Persians* were also. Each chorus must have had a sufficiently obvious type of mask to prevent them in any way from becoming involved with the main actors in the play.

CHARACTER TYPES

According to the fifth-century illustrations, then, the masks were not larger than life. They fitted the head closely and left no room for padding, for they not only covered the face but carried the ornate hair styles or headdress peculiar to the part played by the actor at that particular time. Thus a woman would appear with her hair dressed in the latest fashion if she were meant to represent a woman of fashion, or with her hair shorn if she were a character in mourning (e.g. Electra), with a crown or coronet if she were a queen, possibly with a flowing veil to cover her neck and shoulders, or with other useful defining headdress. Masks of old men were made with bald heads or long untidy white hair, and the masks of young men had flowing locks, carefully arranged or rolled up in the manner of fighting warriors.

A dramatic gesture that could be made was that of changing a mask to represent the same character under different circumstances. A frightening instance of this occurs in the *Oedipus Rex* when after he has stabbed his eyes Oedipus appears before the horrified audience in another mask bearing the same features with blood streaming from the sightless sockets. The same occasion arises during the performance of Euripides' *Cyclops.*

There were, of course, other types of masks to represent unearthly beings. Of these we have little information, but a well-designed mask, as I have already mentioned, could give an awful sense of terror to any audience. Such was the reputation of the Furies [mythical creatures who hunted down murderers] as they appear in Aeschylus' *Eumenides* that boys died of fright and women miscarried. The *Bacchanals* of Euripides are also described as having a terrifying appearance. They were wearing snakes and vine-leaves in their hair, which they had let down in their ecstasy. Other unearthly beings would, of course, include Io with horns and the Okeanids in *Prometheus;* the latter were water nymphs and probably wore their hair flowing. The satyr masks followed a convention of their own. There are so many illustrations of these creatures that there is little doubt that the masks worn to distinguish them were endowed with the same peculiarities. The skull was enlarged in front so that the forehead projected over the eyes, the exact opposite to what was considered classic beauty. The hair receded to baldness on top, showing the full roundness of the skull. There was black hair at the back of the head and a curly black beard. The nose was short and wide and the nostrils distended; the eyes slightly slanting up at the sides and the eyebrows pointed in an expression of permanent surprise. The ears were animal and pressed forward with tufts of hair on the top. Sometimes tiny horns are indicated as on the head of Pan. The forehead has slightly pathetic lines etched on it which give the whole face a curious attraction in spite of its ugliness.

What is particularly interesting about such heads is that the hair follows the prevailing fashions of the day. It is some- times done up at the back in the bound cup-handle shape, a style normally used by young women. This is particularly incongruous when the back of the neck is shown . . . with fat and ageing creases. . . . It is interesting to note that such fifth-century drawings almost without exception show the hair uncut. So much was this habit adhered to that even satyrs and centaurs are depicted in this contemporary style.

Masks of the old comedy of Aristophanes must have in- cluded birds, frogs and wasps; such beings had been illus- trated by the archaic painters and by the Egyptians several centuries earlier, and we are at liberty to use our own imagi- nation in this particular. They need not have been realistic, though certainly they must have been recognizable. We know that the masks worn by the chorus in the *Clouds* represented women (with noses), for this is discussed in the play.

Scenery and Mechanical Devices Heightened Dramatic Effect

James T. Allen

Apparently classical Greek playwright/managers did not employ movable painted scenery as their modern counterparts do. Sophocles, Euripides, and their colleagues did, however, employ painted backdrops and other scenic effects, as well as various kinds of mechanical devices to make their productions more vivid and entertaining. James T. Allen, a former professor of Greek at the University of California, surveys these effects and devices in the following essay.

The Greek theatre . . . evolved from a circular orchestra [area on which plays were staged]; chorus and actors at first occupied the orchestra. Even after the erection of a scene-building the orchestra-area continued to be used by actors as well as chorus throughout the remainder of the fifth century, probably until after the beginning of the Hellenistic period, possibly even until the Roman era. There is no incontestable evidence of a stage in the Greek theatre until at the earliest about 150 B.C., though it is only fair to state that some scholars believe that there was a low platform even as early as the fifth century. . . .

DECORATING THE SCENE-BUILDING

At first there was no scenery. At the time of its introduction and for long afterward scene-painting must have been of a simple, conventional sort. Perhaps it was not scene-painting at all in the modern sense of the term, but merely adornment of the scene-building. However this may be, certainly . . . in the fifth century B.C. the Greeks had nothing compa-

Excerpted from James T. Allen, *Stage Antiquities of the Greeks and Romans and Their Influence* (New York: Cooper Square, 1963). (Endnotes in the original have been omitted in this reprint.)

rable to our modern illusionistic painting. True, in the *Ion* (c. 412 B.C.) of Euripides, the scene of which is laid before the temple of Apollo at Delphi, the chorus in a long passage (*vss.* 184–218) admire the sculptures that adorn the shrine. There is Heracles with golden scimiter slaying the Lernaean hydra, Iolaus "uplifting a flame-wrapped torch."

> *Lo, lo, this other behold*
> *Who rideth a winged horse, dealing death*
> *To a dragon that vomiteth fiery breath,*
> *A monster of shape threefold.*
> *O yea, mine eyes turn swiftly on all . . .*
> *But O, see there on the marble wall*
> *The battle rout of the giant horde!*

Quite unwarranted however is the assumption that this passage affords evidence of elaborate and even realistic scene-painting in the days of Euripides. In so vast a theatre minutiae [small details] of composition would be lost upon the unaided eye. Like the seashore in the *Philoctetes* [by Sophocles, and] the darkness and mud in the *Frogs* [by Aristophanes] . . . these adornments in the *Ion* were no doubt left to the imagination. . . .

But before the close of the Hellenistic era the art of the scene-painter had made great progress and during the Roman period attained a high degree of realism especially in the representation of architectural features. What it was like may be seen in the numerous wall-paintings of Pompeii [the Roman city destroyed and buried by a volcanic eruption in A.D. 79]. . . .

TYPICAL SETTINGS

The settings for plays both Greek and Roman may be divided roughly into four classes. In the first of these there is either no back-scene, as in the *Suppliants* of Aeschylus and perhaps also in his *Persians,* or, if present, it is not used for entrances and exits, but represents a hill or other eminence, or else is entirely ignored. Thus for the *Oedipus Coloneus* of Sophocles the setting is a sacred grove; for the fragmentary *Andromeda* of Euripides, a cliff bordering on the sea. In the second type the scene is a stretch of wild country with rocks, trees and bushes, and a single entrance at the rear representing the mouth of a cavern or hollow rock, as in the *Cyclops* of Euripides, the *Birds* of Aristophanes, and the *Philoctetes* of Sophocles. In the last the orchestra is imagined to be the shore of Lemnos; the background, a desolate hillside with a grotto part way up the slope to which a path leads from the beach below. In the third class the *skene* represents a building: a palace, a temple, a house, a hut, and the like, as occasion demands. Usually in such cases only one door in the back-scene is required. In a few instances, however, two doors are so used, and occasionally even three. Examples are the *Agamemnon* of Aeschylus, the *Alcestis* of Euripides, the *Wasps* of Aristophanes, and many others. Lastly the set is a series of houses or other structures, two or three in number ranged side by side, as in the *Andromache* of Euripides, the *Clouds* of Aristophanes, [and] the *Epitrepontes* of Menander. . . .

CHANGING SCENES

Changes of the set during the progress of a play were of rare occurrence; changes of the scene or locality, frequent. Of the latter the greater number were facilitated by the use of a multiple set, or else depended merely upon the suggestiveness of word and action and the visualizing power of the imagination. . . .

Thus in the *Frogs* of Aristophanes the orchestra represents at first the road and an open space before the house of Heracles. Suddenly Charon, grim ferryman of the dead, appears rowing his tiny boat, and in a twinkling the orchestra becomes a lake. The presence of the boat and Dionysus' exclamation "Why, that's a lake, by Zeus!" are alone sufficient to whisk the imagination of the audience to the Acherusian shores. With the disappearance of Charon and his boat the lake is forgotten, and the orchestra becomes in turn the regions of the dead, dark and loathsome. Again the poet waves his wand, and darkness and mud give place to light most beautiful, and verdant meadows and groves of glossy myrtle, where the blessed "initiates" dance and sing in joyous revelry. Another shift, and Dionysus and his slave stand at the portals of Pluto's dwelling. Similar imagined changes of scene occur in many dramas, more particularly in the older period.

Whenever the setting was altered between plays or within plays, as in the *Eumenides* of Aeschylus and the *Ajax* of Sophocles, this was done in the case of the Greek theatre in full view of the audience. There was no curtain, nor is there the slightest trustworthy evidence for the use of flats [movable pieces of scenery]. . . .

The *Eccyclema*

In an amusing passage in one of the early comedies of Aristophanes, the *Acharnians* (425 B.C.), the leading character, Dicaeopolis, comes to the house of the tragic poet Euripides and as he pounds upon the door calls in a loud voice: "Euripides, dear Rippy! Answer my summons, if ever you answered any man! 'Tis I, Dicaeopolis of Cripplegate!" From within comes the response: "But I'm not at leisure." "At least be wheeled out!" shouts back Dicaeopolis. "Well," replies Euripides, "I'll have myself wheeled out" (*vss.* 403 ff.). Thereupon the doors are thrown open and the poet is wheeled out apparently reclining on a couch. The ensuing dialogue, one of the most diverting in all the pages of Aristophanes, Euripides brings to an abrupt end with the remark: "The fellow is insolent; shut the door!" (*vs.* 479). There is a similar scene in the *Thesmophoriazusae* (c. 411 B.C.), except that in this case the tragic poet Agathon is the butt of the fun, though Euripides, who is present, is himself also held up to ridicule. Agathon suddenly terminates the scene with the command: "Let some one wheel me in at once!"(*vss.* 95 ff., 265).

In these two passages Aristophanes employs with comic effect a contrivance used in the Greek theatre to disclose interior scenes, and known as an *eccyclema,* "that which is rolled out," or *exostra,* "that which is thrust forth." The ancient descriptions of this curious device are confused. It is sometimes spoken of in such a way as to suggest a wheeled platform which could be pushed out through a door; at other times it is referred to as a wheeled and *revolving* platform. More than this we do not know, except that it was used by Aristophanes to heighten his ridicule of Euripides. Naturally modern opinion is divided. Some believe that the *eccyclema* was a semi-circular platform attached to a portion of the front wall of the scene-building and the whole revolved about a pivot after the manner of a butterfly valve; others, that it was a trundle-platform. A third view is that both types were used, the former until about 430 B.C., the latter during the closing decades of the fifth century and later. Equally divergent are the theories regarding the extent to which the *eccyclema* was employed. The extreme conservatives accepting the statements of the scholiasts assume its general use by Aeschylus and Sophocles as well as by Euripides and Aristophanes, not to mention the host of poets whose plays have been lost. The extreme radicals, on the other hand . . .

reject the *eccyclema* except when the evidence in its favor is overwhelming. Between these two positions there is every shade of opinion.

Whatever the truth in the matter, the need of such a contrivance singularly emphasizes for us the limitations of the Greek theatre. In the lack of suitable arrangements for showing interiors the playwrights were compelled to present imaginary interiors out of doors. The effect must have been much the same as that on the Elizabethan stage when various articles of furniture were brought out to suggest an inner scene as is indicated by such stage directions as "a bed thrust out," "enter Elizabeth in her bed," etc. The audience of Shakespeare, like that of Euripides, doubtless accepted the convention with entire complaisance.

There was however another and more natural way of suggesting inner scenes which appears to have been extensively employed both in the Greek and Roman theatres. This was by means of a *prothyron* or portico (Latin *vestibulum*). The opening scene of the *Orestes* of Euripides shows us Electra at the bedside of her brother who has been desperately ill for five days. Similarly in the *Clouds* of Aristophanes (*vss.* 1 ff.) Strepsiades is lying on his couch trying to sleep. Nearby snores Phidippides under a mountain of blankets; the servants too are snoring. It is night time; the lamp sputters and goes out. These are plainly bedroom scenes, yet they are staged out of doors, apparently in the portico. Many other examples occur in the dramas of the fifth century. . . .

How the portico was represented is not known. In the period when the *proskenion* was in use as a background the removal of a few panels from between the columns probably sufficed.

OTHER MECHANICAL DEVICES

In addition to the various mechanical devices which have been described many others were in use in the ancient theatre. Their names and descriptions may be found in the larger treatises. The chief ancient authority is the lexicographer Pollux of the second century A.D. But unfortunately his meaning is not always clear, he often exhibits a most exasperating indifference to chronological sequence, and not infrequently converts a specific instance into a general practice. In spite of these defects, however, his book is of great value and . . . exercised a considerable influence upon the theatre during the period of the Renaissance. He speaks of subterranean stairs, which he calls Charonian steps, for the use of ghosts and other apparitions, trap-doors, devices for imitating thunder and lightning, the *eccyclema*, and several other contrivances, among them the "machine."

The machine, known also as the "crane," was an arrangement by means of which actors could be suspended in the air or lifted to the upper part of the scene-building or lowered from a height to the level of the orchestra or swept across the scene. Thus in the *Peace* of Aristophanes Trygaeus straddles a huge dung-beetle and flies upward to the abode of Zeus. In the lost *Bellerophon* of Euripides the hero, we are told, mounted from earth to heaven on the back of the winged steed Pegasus. In the *Clouds* of Aristophanes Socrates is discovered suspended in a basket, and with mock profundity announces: "I tread the air and contemplate the sun." The contrivance employed in these and similar scenes is said to have been placed at one side high up above the *skene*, but as to the manner in which it was operated there is no definite information. Probably it resembled an ordinary crane.

The date when the machine was added to the appurtenances of the theatre is not known. Some ascribe it to Euripides; others quite as confidently to Aeschylus. That, however, it was often employed by Euripides and Aristophanes is beyond question, especially by the former for introducing a god at the close of a play to make an epilogic pronouncement . . . or to untangle a situation that has become too intricate. From its frequent use for the latter purpose particularly by inferior dramatists arose the familiar expression "a god from the machine" (*deus ex machina*). An interesting parallel to this is found in the French *Les Miracles de Notre Dame* and the German *Marienspiele*, in which time and time again the Blessed Virgin appears to rescue a favorite from some dire predicament. Parallels occur also in the drama of modern times.

CHAPTER 2

Greek Tragedy

Greek
Drama

The Nature of Tragedy

D.W. Lucas

In this enlightening essay, D.W. Lucas, formerly of King's College and Cambridge University, discusses the general tone and structure of Greek tragedy, at times citing Aristotle, who composed an extensive analysis of the genre in the fourth century B.C. Lucas also conveniently identifies the major components, literary devices, and effects of typical Greek tragedies (although, as he points out, all of these things were not necessarily to be found in every tragedy). These include: the *hamartia*, or tragic error committed by the hero; the *peripeteia*, an unexpected turn of events that brings that error to the fore; the *anagnorisis*, the hero's recognition of his error; and *catharsis*, a release of emotional tension (or an emotional cleansing) generated by watching a tragedy.

It is well for anyone who proposes to describe and criticize tragedies to make clear from the start what meaning he attaches to the word tragedy. . . . To an Athenian anything was a tragedy which was produced at the tragic contests and was not a satyr-play. To us the word suggests a serious play with an unhappy ending. Accordingly we must accept under the heading of Greek tragedy a number of plays with more or less happy endings, a few of which, notably the *Helen* [by Euripides], are not conspicuously serious. Aristotle, whom it is impossible to keep out of this discussion, regarded plays with unhappy endings as the most truly tragic. He would no doubt have justified the inclusion of serious plays with happy endings on the ground that they arouse, at least during part of their performance, the same emotions of pity and fear as a play with an unhappy ending. . . . All the same we are justified in regarding tragedy in the modern sense as significantly different from any play that ends happily because it contains an assertion that men in this world can be over-

taken by undeserved catastrophe. Not every one would admit that catastrophe is really the last word, but the end of
tragedy is apparent catastrophe, and it is one out of propor-
tion to the deserts of the sufferers, because the mere fact that
the play is serious makes it unlikely that the characters will
be so worthless that they may be said to deserve all they get.
None the less the degree of guilt attaching to them may vary
greatly between tragedy and tragedy. We need only compare
[Shakespeare's] *Macbeth* and *Othello.*

ARISTOTLE'S VIEW OF TRAGEDY

It is open to question how far tragedies of different periods
and different societies can be judged by the same standards.
The Greek tragic form certainly has many peculiarities of its
own, not least important its comparative brevity. Aristotle
had read far more Greek drama than we ever shall, and is allowed even by those who admire him least to have possessed
remarkable powers of generalizing, so that it is natural to
start from his account. But it should be remembered that in
making his generalizations he took little account of Aeschylus, and that he seems to have regarded the heroic legends
which were the raw material of tragedy with an indifference
in no way characteristic of the previous century when the
tragedies were composed.

Tragedy, says Aristotle, is a representation of a serious action performed by characters sufficiently like us to arouse our
sympathy but better than we are. The action shows the
change in the hero's fortunes, a change in the best type of
tragedy from good to bad. The unity of the play depends on
there being a causal connection between the episodes of the
play such that we are shown a series of events each of which
is a necessary or probable consequence of what has gone before. With this demand for logic and emphasis on causality is
connected the famous claim that poetry is more philosophical
than history; logic is the same on the stage as in the world,
and the logical connections between actions and events can
be revealed more clearly in the simplified relations of drama
than in the complex confusions of real life, where the forces
involved are more numerous and less calculable.

In order that this sequence of events may be necessary or
probable the hero, unless he is a purely passive victim, must
himself take the initial step. Since this step will lead eventually to catastrophe it will usually be taken in ignorance of

the consequences. This is the celebrated *hamartia;* it may be both mistaken and wrong, as it was in the case of Ajax; more often it is only mistaken, as with Oedipus, whether we regard his error as being his misconception of his parents' identity or his actions in killing a man who turned out to be his father and marrying a woman who was his mother. And here the error is the more striking in that Oedipus, in consequence of the oracle, was trying to avoid doing these very things. This brings us to what, in Aristotle's view, were two very important features of a well constructed play, *peripeteia* and *anagnorisis,* or recognition. If the hero begins the action under a misapprehension a moment must come, often just before the catastrophe, when he realizes his mistake and its consequences, and the situation is then transformed. Since it frequently happens in Greek tragedy that the vital misapprehension relates to the identity of one of the characters, recognitions are an important feature and often coincide with the *peripeteia.* At the climax of the *Oedipus,* the hero recognizes himself as the son of Laius and his wife as his own mother.

Of the hero Aristotle has little to say; he has indeed no word to describe him. He is merely the character who experiences a change of fortune. For although the action arises out of some initiative of the hero's, the course the action takes is not, in most plays, closely connected with the hero's personality, and even his original initiative is often a response to a force intruding from outside. . . .

COMING FACE TO FACE WITH CATASTROPHE

The emotions aroused by tragedy are largely painful. Why do we of our own free will expose ourselves to this pain? To this question there is not, and there is not likely to be, an agreed answer. The reactions of an audience at a dramatic performance are complex, and individuals vary widely in their responses. Accordingly it is a mistake to seek . . . a single answer to this problem. In the first place we like excitement, and our faculty of readily identifying ourselves with one of the parties to a contest, whether a football team or a dramatic hero, makes this emotion easily accessible. In excitement there is liable to be an element of pain. It is a price which the young especially, the class which according to Plato is most addicted to tragedy, are ready to pay. Excitement is often present in high tragedy, though a drama which offers no more than excitement is merely melodrama. Yet there is little in the *Poetics* which is not a recipe as much for melodrama as for tragedy; the technical devices on which Aristotle lavishes most careful attention belong as much to one as to the other, and there remains a doubt whether he was not more fascinated by what the *Oedipus Rex* has in common with melodrama than by the qualities which raise it to a higher level.

But the tragic character, little though the Greeks had to say about him, is something more than the victim of exciting vicissitudes [variations]. His full stature can be revealed only in adversity; that is why tragedy has to be tragic. Only when the difficulties are most overwhelming, the threat of catastrophe overpowering, can his potentialities be realized. Quality can not be known in the last resort except through the ordeal that tests it. Nor is it right to think of action and character in isolation, because it is in relation to the action that the character is conceived; unfortunately it is rarely possible to talk about anything without separating it from other things with which it is in fact united.

Nearly everyone is prepared to risk some pain for the sake of excitement; many people are ready to undergo a sharper pain in order to share the vision of human greatness at full stretch which the tragic poet can communicate. Again we need not be particularly surprised. The literature of catastrophe has always been highly popular. We have a natural curiosity about the behaviour of ordinary people in extraordinary situations. One of the humbler functions of literature is to widen our knowledge, to increase our emotional range, and to enrich our lives with vicarious experience. Most of us, so far, have not come face to face with the more spectacular forms of catastrophe, with shipwreck, plague, or conflagration. We naturally wonder how people behave, how we should behave, in the circumstances. Fewer, but still a large number, wonder how human beings of a higher temper would behave in trials still more terrible. Tragedy can show the very extreme of human grandeur.

EMOTIONAL RELEASE

It is a common experience to find that the emotional stress of seeing a tragedy is followed by a sense of calm and tranquillity: 'calm of mind, all passion spent'; or again, 'what may quiet us in a death so noble'. That this should be so is not surprising. The emotional experience may be intense, but it ends abruptly at, or soon after, the fall of the curtain, whereas the disasters of real life continue to cast their shadow for months and years. It is not strange that the easing of emotional strain should be noticeable and agreeable. However, far-reaching conclusions have been drawn from this effect of tragedy, usually in connection with Aristotle's theory of *catharsis*, which [English epic poet John] Milton had in mind when he wrote the phrases quoted above. That the effect of tragedy is cathartic is still for many the starting point for all consideration of the subject. . . .

A more hazardous inference from the sense of calm and reconciliation which may follow the seeing or reading of tragedy is that the reconciliation may be implicit in the tragedy itself, as a true picture, so far as it goes, of the universe, that behind the apparent tragedy there is harmony and that somewhere, somehow, good is triumphant. When such a vindication of the universe is part of the writer's purpose and grows out of his belief, we may no doubt be left with a sense of the higher harmony. But such a play will hardly be a tragedy in the normal sense of the word; this is very relevant to the tragedies of Aeschylus, which often end with reconciliation. It is in the nature of tragedy that it should raise, directly or indirectly, the problem of divine justice. The answer may not be a denial, but it will not be a confident affirmation. Hence the question has been raised, and variously answered, whether tragedy is possible, in the full sense of the word, within a system of Christian belief. . . . It is not, since to the Christian, as to Plato, success and disaster are things not very momentous, and a drama that reaches its conclusion in this world cannot be complete. The only real tragedy is the tragedy of the lost soul.

TRAGEDY: A COMMENTARY ON LIFE

Akin to this is the question how far the tragic poet was, of set purpose, a teacher. It is commonly asserted that he was, but this assertion has called forth contradiction; the idea that tragedy is a didactic [instructive] art can arouse distaste. Possibly Aristophanes' famous line, 'Boys have a master to teach them, but the teachers of men are poets' (*Frogs* 1055), has been too freely quoted. Many of the claims made for the instructiveness of poetry both in the *Frogs* and in Plato's *Ion* are pretty ridiculous. Yet such claims were an attempt to rationalize the general feeling that poetry was important, and poets wise. If this had not been widely believed Socrates would not have turned to the poets in the expectation of finding men wiser than himself (*Apology* 22B). But about the middle of the fifth century the poets began to suffer from the competition of other and more professional teachers. By the end of the century poetry was coming to be regarded mainly as entertainment. For Aristotle the theatre was a source of pleasure, salutary pleasure it is true; and though he allowed poetry to be more philosophical than history, he certainly thought it a great deal less philosophical than philosophy. Yet so far as the ordinary man was concerned, for long it was the poets who discoursed on fundamental problems of human suffering and divine justice, who delivered the homilies which no one in the ancient world expected from a priest. Indeed, in any age to touch on the ultimate mysteries without in a sense teaching is not possible for a poet who takes his work seriously. A tragedy by its very nature is a commentary on life. But all this is very far from meaning that the poet began from an edifying idea which he worked up into a play. It means that the play would be set within a framework of accepted ideas which would receive fresh strength and significance from the play. And it was not without relevance that it was performed in honour of a god and in a place sacred to him on an occasion of great solemnity.

Sophocles' *Antigone* Explores Western Cultural Ideals

Victor D. Hanson and John Heath

Many of the masterpieces of fifth-century B.C. Greek drama have as their themes political, social, and cultural concepts and ideals that are peculiarly Greek and which have, over time, become a part of Western civilization's fabric. Noted classicists Victor D. Hanson, of California State University at Fresno, and John Heath, of Santa Clara University, here single out and examine such concepts and ideals from the text of Sophocles' play *Antigone*, the renowned story of a woman who challenges the authority of her city's ruler by disobeying his order to leave her brother's body unburied.

The answer to why the world is becoming Westernized goes all the way back to the wisdom of the Greeks.... Our own implicit principles and values can be rediscovered in ... Sophocles' tragedy *Antigone* (441 B.C.), produced at the zenith of Athenian imperial power and cultural hegemony. Within a mere 1,353 lines one can detect most of the cultural assumptions of all the Greeks that we now 2,500 years later take for granted—even though Sophocles' tragedy is an exploration of civic and private morality, *not* a treatise on culture. In other words, a piece of Athenian literature, otherwise ostensibly *unconcerned* with political science or cultural studies, can serve as an effective primer to anyone curious about how we are like the Greeks in our daily lives. If we put aside for a moment the *Antigone* as great literature and examine the nuts and bolts of its underlying assumptions about man and culture, the play can be as revealing from the values it presumes as from the tensions it raises and the ideas it challenges.

BACKGROUND NOISES OF THE DRAMA

The play's heroine is Antigone, sister and daughter of the dead Oedipus. She opposes a royal edict forbidding burial of her brother, Polyneices, the defeated usurper of Thebes, who had tried to wrest the kingdom from his own brother. Forced either to follow the law or her own notions of universal morality and sisterly duty, Antigone attempts to give burial rites to Polyneices. This pious but illegal act earns her a death sentence. A Sophoclean calamity follows for her uncle, the regent king Creon, who would punish her for traitorous conduct. Creon's increasingly tyrannical behavior in pursuit of the law—fear and rejection of family, fellow citizens, and the divine—results in the death of his son, his wife, and Antigone herself. The state and its smug assurance that statute can challenge divinely inspired custom seem to go too far, with disastrous consequences for all involved.

Within this single drama—in great part, a harsh critique of Athenian society and the Greek city-state in general—Sophocles tells of the eternal struggle between the state and the individual, human and natural law, and the enormous gulf between what we attempt here on earth and what fate has in store for us all. In this magnificent dramatic work, almost incidentally so, we find nearly every reason why we are now what we are. The following categories taken from the play by no means exhaust the Western paradigm [pattern of cultural ideas and principles]. They are, again, *not* even the chief reasons to read the tragedy; they are simply the background noises of the drama. These underlying cultural assumptions, however . . . illuminate much about our own lives in the West at the turn of the millennium.

THE PRICE OF PROGRESS

To the Greeks, the free exchange of ideas, the abstract and rational inquiry about the physical and material world, and the pursuit of knowledge for its own sake create a dynamic that is both brilliant and frightening at the same time—and unlike that of any other culture. The chorus of Theban elders in a triumphant ode sing of the progress of technology in its mastery over nature. There are "many wondrous things and nothing more wondrous than man," whose naval, agricultural, medical, and manufacturing sciences have conquered everything but death itself. Armed with his dangerous "inventive craft," *polis* man—that is, the citizen of the city-state—can apply his mechanical skill (*techné*) "beyond all expectation," and use it "for either evil or good," a potent scientific enterprise whose goal is progress itself at any cost. It is no wonder that the troubled Sophocles chooses to use the ambiguous adjective *deina* for "wondrous." The Greek word is more akin to the English "awful," or "formidable" and means both wonderful and terrible—astonishingly good *or* strange and unusual to the point of being terribly bad.

To Sophocles, who experienced the splendor and precipitous decline of imperial Athens in the fifth century, and who recognized the role of both divine fate and mortal hubris in its descent, there is always a price to be paid for relentless human progress that, in [his playwright colleague] Euripides' words, makes "us arrogant in claiming that we are better than the Gods." Anyone who has witnessed our mountains denuded of primeval forests so that the lower middle classes might have clean, affordable, and durable tract houses recognizes the technological and ethical trade-off that Sophocles worried about.

QUESTIONING MILITARY AUTHORITY

Throughout the *Antigone*, the would-be usurper Polyneices is condemned for raising an army outside the law to gain control of Thebes. Moreover, Creon's guards serve not as retainers—who may bolt and change sides when their king's fortunes wane—but rather as reluctant militiamen who enforce legislation that they do not necessarily like. Nowhere is their "general" a divine prince. These men-at-arms therefore can freely offer advice, even speak rudely if need be, to their commander-in-chief, who exercises power solely by his position as the legal head of the state. The Guard, in fact, rebukes Creon for his rash and unsubstantiated charges: "How terrible to guess, and to guess at untruths!" Sophocles was writing within a society where almost every elected Greek general was at some time either fined, exiled, ostracized, or executed, where almost every commander fought beside his men and hardly a one survived when his army did not. The playwright himself both led men into battle and served as auditor of others who had failed. No one in Sophocles' audience would have thought it at all strange for a soldier to question his leader or for a lowly private to be a wiser man than his general. As Aristotle reminds us of Athens, "All offices connected with the military are to be elected by an open vote."

THE CONSEQUENCES OF CONSTITUTIONAL GOVERNMENT

The idea of constitutional government permeates every aspect of the *Antigone*. Although the Greek tragedians anachronistically use the conventions of early myth and thus the dramatic architecture from the pre–city-state world of kings and clans, much of the *Antigone* is about contradictions within law, government, and jurisprudence—issues very much at stake in Sophocles' own fifth-century world of Athens. The poet transforms the mythical monarchy of Thebes into a veritable contemporary city-state, where citizens must make legislation and yet live with that majority decision even when it is merely legal and not at all ethical or moral. Creon must announce the edict "to the whole people." Antigone and her sister Ismene acknowledge that burying their brother and thus breaking the law of the *polis* is illegal and therefore "against the citizens." When Creon boasts of his power to enforce the state's edict, his own son Haemon is made to counter, "No *polis* is the property of a single man." No city-state—even the more oligarchical—really was.

Creon himself turns out to be a tragic figure, an utterly Western rational creature who devotes himself to the law above every other human and divine concern. He is tragic in his own right not just because he goes against the moral consensus of his own citizenry and the wishes of the gods, but because he does so in the sincere belief that as head of state he is adhering to a necessary Greek sense of consensual government—something which exists only, in Aristotle's words, "when the citizens rule and are then ruled in turn."

RELIGION IS SEPARATE FROM AND
SUBORDINATE TO POLITICAL AUTHORITY

In the Greek city-state, no high priest is invested with absolute political authority. This separation of roles will . . . establish an ideal that would serve reformers for the next two and a half millennia. The council and assembly govern political and military affairs—stage elections, vote on legislation, appoint generals, call out the militias, expect the citizens, not the state, to provide arms. In the age of the classical city-state, no free citizen curtsies or kowtows to a living deity. Prophets, seers, and priests conduct festivals, sacrifices, advise, counsel, and interpret the supernatural; they do not *per se* direct state policy or override the will of the assembly. The archon is not God incarnate, who marries his sister, leads his people in public prayer and sacrifice, oversees the building of his monumental tomb, or sits on a peacock throne. The holy man may threaten or mesmerize in his attempts to sway the assembly, but sway the assembly he must.

Thus in the *Antigone*, the seer Teiresias, who through his supernatural craft possesses greater wisdom than Creon, nevertheless is slandered ("The whole pack of seers is money-mad") and arbitrarily dismissed by the king. When he is told to leave, he goes. It is not Creon's sacrilegious abuse of the holy man Teiresias that dooms him; rather it is his paranoia and political extremism in rejecting the sound, rational advice of family and friend alike. No Greek would think that Teiresias deserved a veto or that Creon could read the signs of birds. Plato saw the holy man and the statesman as distinct; "the diviner arrogant with pride and influence" was not to intrude into government, "as in Egypt, where the King cannot rule unless he has the power of a priest."

FAITH IN THE AVERAGE CITIZEN

The yeoman farmer, the shepherd, the small craftsmen, the nurse, the citizen-soldier—these are the unsung heroes of Greek tragic and comic drama. These secondary but essential characters and chorus members provide the stable backdrop for the murder, incest, and madness of a royal and divine mythical elite who live in a different world from the rest of us. At the very origins of Western culture, Greece created an anti-aristocratic ethos often hostile to the accumulation of riches, and to the entire notion of the wealthy man of influence—and it is one of the few societies in the history of civilization to have done so.

The Greeks were more naturally suspicious than admiring of plutocratic hierarchy, indeed of anything that threatened the decentralized nature of the *polis*, which is the natural expression of a community of peers. Haemon warns his father Creon of the public rumbling over Antigone's death sentence, of the need to consider the opinion of the "common man," "the people who share our city." In the *Antigone* of Sophocles (himself the well-born son of a wealthy manufacturer), the populist streak runs strong in almost every direction—economic, social, and political. Creon himself rails against the power of money: "You will see more people destroyed than saved by dirty profits." Earlier he had concluded, "Men are ruined by the hope of profit."

Both Sophocles and Euripides endow their middling messengers, guards, farmers, heralds, caretakers, and shepherds with a refreshing degree of common sense; they are wily, astute, sensitive, rarely naive, rarely buffoons. The messenger in the *Antigone* dryly concludes of the royal fiasco, "Enjoy your wealth; live the life of a king; but once your enjoyment has left, these are but the shadows of smoke in comparison to lost happiness." No wonder the play ends with, "Great words of the haughty bring great blows upon them"—words that would have cost a Persian of those times his head. In short, Sophocles was drawing on a rich anti-aristocratic tradition of the previous two centuries . . . [that revels in] exposing the ugly side of the rich and famous. Sophocles' contemporary Thucydides has Athenagoras say of the people's ability to govern that the wealthy are fit only as guardians of property, while "the many, they are the best judges of what is spoken."

THE POWER AND PERILS OF A FREE MARKET

In the world of the Greek city-state, the citizen has title to his own property, the right to inherit and to pass on what is rightfully his. That decentralized system explains why the Greeks colonized—and often exploited—the Eastern and southern Mediterranean rather than vice versa. But in contrast to the earlier palatial dynasties to the East and South, taxation and the forced labor of the free citizenry were nearly nonexistent. Creon, like so many Greek rightists from the sixth-century B.C. aristocrat Theognis to Plato, railed against the rise of capital and commerce among the citizenry, which had destroyed the allocation of wealth and power by birth alone, to the detriment of his own inherited, entrenched position: "No practice is as pernicious among the citizenry as coined money. It destroys the state; it drives men from their homes; it teaches men vice in order to abandon good sense in favor of shameful deeds." Wealth without proof of morality upsets static norms of social behavior and established political power, disrupting old hierarchies as well as the obedience and compliance of the populace.

In short, the free market—even the Greeks' less-developed, protocapitalist one—erodes inherited privilege, allowing a different and changeable standard of merit, based on achievement, to prevail. When Athenian democracy is either scorned by the Old Oligarch (the name given to the author of a fifth-century treatise denouncing Athenian democracy) or praised by Pericles himself, the focus is often on the harbor and agora, the loci of free trade and commerce which empower the mob and give flesh to the abstract promise of equality.

FREE SPEECH AND ACTS OF DISSENT

Anywhere else in the Mediterranean the loud-mouthed, hell-raising troublemaker is shunned, beheaded, or transmogrified into the court toady. In the Greek world the dissident—Ajax, Philoctetes, Lysistrata, Electra, Prometheus [title characters of famous ancient Greek plays]—often becomes the eponymous hero of the play. Antigone attacks Greek culture on a variety of fronts—the tyranny of the state over the individual, the mindless chauvinism of a male supremacist, the complacence and passivity of timid citizenry, the relativism of a more modern world growing insidiously in her midst. She warns that no mortal, even with the law of the state at his side, "could trample down the unwritten and unfailing laws of the gods." Head-to-head in a moral debate with Creon, she pushes the king to the shallow refuge of sexual bias. Exasperated, he can only bluster: "No woman rules me while I live." When Antigone's more circumspect and fence-sitting sister Ismene finally decides to participate in the burial, she receives from Antigone a cold "No": "I cannot love a friend whose love is words."

One could argue that Sophocles himself wants to undermine the very *polis* that allows him to present his dramas, that he uses his state subsidy to convince his Athenian patrons that their problem, the cause of their decline, is in *them*, not in the gods, women, foreigners, slaves, or other Greeks. His contemporary Pericles says of such free speech that it is "not a stumbling block but rather a vital precursor for any action at all."

Women in Greek Tragedy Versus Real Greek Women

Sarah B. Pomeroy

*This insightful tract is excerpted from the widely ac-
claimed book* Goddesses, Whores, Wives, and Slaves:
Women in Classical Antiquity *by Sarah B. Pomeroy, a
professor of Classics at Hunter College. She makes
the point that it is not legitimate to reconstruct the
lives of real fifth-century* B.C. *Greek women solely
based on observations of female characters in the
period's surviving plays. After exploring some of the
reasons for the depictions of strong, larger-than-life
women in the plays of Aeschylus, Sophocles, and
Euripides, Pomeroy concludes that some of these
characters' attributes reflected the reality of the day,
while others were clearly exaggerated or fictitious.*

If respectable Athenian women were secluded and silent,
how are we to account for the forceful heroines of tragedy
and comedy? And why does the theme of strife between
woman and man pervade Classical drama? Before proceed-
ing to complex explanations which are directly concerned
with women, it is necessary to repeat the truism that the
dramatists examined multiple aspects of man's relationship
to the universe and to society; accordingly, their examina-
tion of another basic relationship—that between man and
woman—is not extraordinary. It is rather the apparent dis-
crepancy between women in the actual society and the heroines on the stage that demands investigation. Several hy-
potheses have been formulated in an attempt to explain the
conflict between fact and fiction.

Many plots of tragedy are derived from myths of the
Bronze Age preserved by epic poets. As we have observed,
the royal women of epic were powerful, not merely within

their own homes but in an external political sense. To the Athenian audience familiar with the works of Homer, not even an iconoclast [rebel against tradition] like Euripides could have presented a silent and repressed Helen or Clytemnestra. Likewise, the Theban epic cycle showed the mutual fratricide of the sons of Oedipus. The surviving members of the family were known to be Antigone and Ismene. Sophocles could not have presented these sisters as boys. In short, some myths that provided the plots of Classical tragedies described the deeds of strong women, and the Classical dramatist could not totally change these facts.

Those who believe in the historical existence of Bronze Age matriarchy also propose an answer to our questions: the male-female polarity discernible in Bronze Age myths can be explained by referring to an actual conflict between a native pre-Hellenic matriarchal society and the patriarchy introduced by conquering invaders.

The Bronze Age origin of these myths does not explain why Athenian tragic poets, living at least seven hundred years later in a patriarchal society, not only found these stories congenial but accentuated the power of their heroines. For example, in the *Odyssey* Aegisthus is the chief villain in the murder of Agamemnon, but in the tragedies of Aeschylus a shift was made to highlight Clytemnestra as the prime mover in the conspiracy. Electra, the daughter of Clytemnestra, is a colorless figure in mythology, and in the *Odyssey* Orestes alone avenges his father; but two dramatists elevated Electra and created whole plays around her and her dilemma. Similarly, Sophocles is thought to have been responsible for the story of the conflict between Creon and Antigone. Homer, it is true, showed how Calypso and Circe could unman even the hero Odysseus, who more easily survived other ordeals, but these two were immortal females. The mortal women in epic, however vital, are not equivalent in impact to tragic heroines, nor is their power such as to produce the male-female conflicts that tragedy poses in a pervasive and demanding way.

Some Women Were Secluded, but Others Were Not

A number of scholars find a direct relationship between real women living in Classical Athens and the heroines of tragedy. They reason that the tragic poets found their models not in the Bronze Age but among the real women known to them. From this theory they deduce that real women were neither secluded nor repressed in Classical times. They use as evidence, for example, the fact that tragic heroines spent much time conversing out-of-doors without worrying about being seen. This argument lacks cogency, since the scenes of tragedy are primarily out-of-doors and female characters could scarcely be portrayed if they had to be kept indoors. The proponents of this argument question how dramatists could have become so familiar with feminine psychology if they never had a chance to be with women. They ignore the fact that playwrights were familiar with their female relatives, as well as with the numerous resident aliens and poor citizen women who did move freely about the city. At least one group of women—the wives of citizens with adequate means—probably was secluded.

It is not legitimate for scholars to make judgments about the lives of real women solely on the basis of information gleaned from tragedy. When an idea expressed in tragedy is supported by other genres of ancient sources, then only is it clearly applicable to real life. Ismene's statement [in Sophocles' *Antigone*] that the proper role of women is not to fight with men can be said to reflect real life, since it agrees with information derived from Classical oratory and from comedy. But when Clytemnestra murders her husband, or Medea her sons, or when Antigone takes credit for an act of civil disobedience, we cannot say that these actions have much to do with the lives of real women in Classical Athens, although isolated precedents in Herodotus could be cited for passionate, aggressive women (including a barbarian queen who contrived the murder of her husband with his successor; another who opposed men in battle; and a third who cut off the breasts, nose, ears, lips, and tongue of her rival's mother). However, as images of women in Classical literature written by men, heroines such as Clytemnestra, Medea, and Antigone are valid subjects for contemplation.

TRAGIC HEROINES BASED ON "REPRESSED MOTHERS"?

Retrospective psychoanalysis has been used to analyze the experience of young boys in Classical Athens, and thus to explain the mature dramatist's depiction of strong heroines. According to the sociologist Philip Slater, the Athenian boy spent his early formative years primarily in the company of his mother and female slaves. The father passed the day away from home, leaving the son with no one to defend him from the mother. The relationship between mother and son was marked by ambiguity and contradiction. The secluded woman nursed a repressed hostility against her elderly, inconsiderate, and mobile husband. In the absence of her husband, the mother substituted the son, alternately pouring forth her venom and doting on him. She demanded that he be successful and lived vicariously through him. The emotionally powerful mother impressed herself upon the imagination of the young boy, becoming the seed, as it were, which developed into the dominant female characters of the mature playwright's mind. The Classical dramatist tended to choose those myths of the Bronze Age that were most fascinating to him, since they explored certain conflicts that existed within his own personality. The "repressed mother" explanation works in inverse ratio to the power of the heroines produced by the son: the more repressed his mother was and the more ambivalent her behavior, the more dreadful were the heroines portrayed by the dramatist-son.

Slater's theory is an interesting attempt to answer a difficult question. Some readers may abhor the interpretation of classical antiquity by means of psychoanalytic approaches. But since the myths of the past illuminate the present, it appears valid to examine them with the critical tools of the present. Still, there are problems with Slater's analysis, just as there were with the more traditional ones. First, although adult Athenians lived sex-segregated lives, it is far from certain that fathers were distant from children. Inferences from the modern "commuting father" have too much influenced Slater's view of antiquity. In fact, comedy shows a closeness between fathers and children: children could accompany fathers when they were invited out, and a father claimed to have nursed a baby and bought toys for him. Second, the reader would have to accept Slater's premise that women constrained in a patriarchal society would harbor rage, whether or not they themselves were aware of it. . . . The epitaphs of women assumed that their lives were satisfactory, although this evidence may be somewhat discounted since the inscriptions were selected by the surviving members of the family, most probably male. But even today many believe that women can find happiness in the role of homemaker, particularly when traditional expectations are being fulfilled. Thus Athenian women may well have lacked the internal conflict of, say, Roman women, who were plagued with the frustrations arising from relative freedom which confronted them with the realm of men, but tantalizingly kept its trophies just beyond their grasp. Is it more reasonable to suggest from a modern viewpoint that the boredom of tasks like constant weaving must have driven Athenian women to insanity, or, in contrast, to call attention to the satisfaction women may have felt at jobs well done?

I am not convinced that we can learn much about the Athenian mother from Slater, but his work is useful for the

MEDEA—A LARGER-THAN-LIFE GREEK WOMAN

The female leads of the great tragedians were often driven to commit outrageous and/or violent acts. This exchange between the title character of Euripides' Medea *and her husband, Jason, takes place directly after she has slain their children to exact revenge against him.*

JASON
O children, what a wicked mother she was to you!

MEDEA
They died from a disease they caught from their father.

JASON
I tell you it was not my hand that destroyed them.

MEDEA
But it was your insolence, and your virgin wedding.

JASON
And just for the sake of that you chose to kill them.

MEDEA
Is love so small a pain, do you think, for a woman?

JASON
For a wise one, certainly. But you are wholly evil.

MEDEA
The children are dead. I say this to make you suffer.

JASON
The children, I think, will bring down curses on you.

MEDEA
The gods know who was the author of this sorrow.

JASON
Yes, the gods know indeed, they know your loathsome heart.

MEDEA
Hate me. But I tire of your barking bitterness.

Quoted in Rex Warner, trans., *Three Great Plays of Euripides.* New York: New American Library, 1958, p. 69.

analysis of the male playwright's creative imagination. For explanations of the powerful women in tragedy, we must look to the poets, and to other men who judged the plays and selected what they thought best. The mythology about women is created by men and, in a culture dominated by men, it may have little to do with flesh-and-blood women. This is not to deny that the creative imagination of the playwright was surely shaped by some women he knew. But it was also molded by the entire milieu of fifth-century Athens, where separation of the sexes as adults bred fear of the unfamiliar; and finally by the heritage of his literary past, including not only epic but Archaic poetry, with its misogynistic [anti-female] element.

Misogyny was born of fear of women. It spawned the ideology of male superiority. But this was ideology, not statement of fact; as such, it could not be confirmed, but was open to constant doubt. Male status was not immutable. Myths of matriarchies and Amazon societies showed female dominance. Three of the eleven extant comedies of Aristophanes show women in successful opposition to men. A secluded wife like Phaedra may yearn for adultery; a wife like Creusa may have borne an illegitimate son before her current marriage; a good wife like Deianira can murder her husband. These were the nightmares of the victors; that some day the vanquished would arise and treat their ex-masters as they themselves had been treated.

Most important, in the period between Homer and the tragedians, the city-state, with established codes of behavior, had evolved, and the place of women as well as of other disenfranchised groups in the newly organized society was an uncomfortable one. Many tragedies show women in rebellion against the established norms of society. As the *Oresteia* of Aeschylus makes clear, a city-state such as Athens flourished only through the breaking of familial or blood bonds and the subordination of the patriarchal family within the patriarchal state. But women were in conflict with this political principle, for their interests were private and family-related. Thus, drama often shows them acting out of the women's quarters, and concerned with children, husbands, fathers, brothers, and religions deemed more primitive and family-oriented than the Olympian, which was the support of the state. This is the point at which the image of the heroine on the stage coincides with the reality of Athenian women.

Euripides' Rejection of Tragic Tradition

Herbert N. Couch

As the late classical scholar Herbert N. Couch explains here, in his plays Euripides often dealt with human emotions in a realistic way, as opposed to Aeschylus and Sophocles, whose characters tended to be larger-than-life. For his day, says Couch, Euripides also showed unusual sympathy for those who suffer from life's tragic twists and turns. And for these reasons he displayed what many view as decidedly modern qualities of expression.

Aeschylus and Sophocles had found in the form of tragedy, which they inherited and enlarged, a fitting vehicle for their art and philosophy. Perhaps they exhausted its potential limits: at any rate, in the career of the next and last great dramatist of the fifth century we find an absence of harmony in the pursuit of his literary work that is in marked contrast with his older associates.

EURIPIDES' LIFE

Euripides was born on the island of Salamis, probably in the year 480 B.C., though it is not necessary to treat too seriously the tradition that the day of his birth coincided with the Battle of Salamis. Some authorities put the year of his birth as early as 485 B.C. In any case, he belongs to a generation distinctly later than that of Aeschylus or Sophocles. The youth of Euripides was spent at the home of his parents in the village of Phlya, near Athens, where, despite the meagerness of evidence relating to his boyhood and the acerbity of Aristophanes' jibes at the poverty and squalor of his early surroundings, there is every reason to believe that he passed the childhood of one to whom many privileges of education and culture were available. He was too young to have known

Excerpted from Herbert N. Couch, *Classical Civilization: Greece* (Englewood Cliffs, NJ: Prentice-Hall, 1940).

anything of the Persian Wars, and by the time that he reached years of understanding, Athens had already entered upon the promise of the fifth century. When Pericles assumed power in 461 B.C., Euripides was but nineteen years of age and had already been engaged for a year or more in the composition of tragedies, although it was not until 455 B.C., when he was twenty-five years old, that he was first able to compete in a dramatic festival. In the following year, 454 B.C., . . . Euripides was in late youth, with his habits of thought already formed by a society that was forgetting the stern traditions of equity that characterized the generation of [the battle of] Marathon [fought against the Persians in 490 B.C.]. The first of the few victories won by Euripides belongs to the year 441 B.C.

Tradition makes Euripides a pupil of Anaxagoras, the philosopher, and Protagoras, the sophist [teacher], the former of whom was driven out of Athens on the charge of religious unorthodoxy in 429 B.C. From such persons as these, as well as from Socrates and the sophist Prodicus, with whom he must surely have associated, Euripides absorbed the questioning and doubting philosophy of the city, which was reflected in the intensity of his attacks on current and accepted beliefs. Though Euripides was apparently but little liked by his contemporaries, his popularity grew in his later years, and there is a pleasing story that many an Athenian soldier taken captive at Syracuse during the military expedition that met defeat in 413 B.C., gained his freedom in return for delighting his Syracusan captors by reciting verses from the plays of Euripides. The poet died in Macedonia in 406 B.C., a few months before the death of his older rival, Sophocles.

SOCIAL PROBLEMS AND OTHER CONTEMPORARY INFLUENCES

Tastes and styles changed rapidly in the fifth century. Aeschylus had written his sonorous verses about themes that lay closer to the lives of the gods than to the daily experience of man; Sophocles had examined some of the moral and ethical problems of his time, but without passionate intensity; Euripides, on the contrary, imparted his own burning conviction on social problems to his plays, but in so doing he attacked the conservative elements in Athens with a ferocity that defeated his own purpose by alienating sympathy. He was touched by philosophic speculation, so that he became more and more uncompromising in his denunciation of injustice.

In further contrast to the peaceful career that was traditionally the lot of Sophocles, Euripides was unhappy in his
home life, unfortunate in his marriage, and during his earlier years intensely unpopular with the citizens of Athens,
whose sufferings he had at heart more than any other
writer of the age. He won but five first prizes in all, one after his death.

Ninety-two plays, presented in the half-century between
455 B.C. and 405 B.C., are attributed to Euripides. Of these,
nineteen have been preserved, if the *Rhesus,* of doubtful au-
thenticity, be included in the list. The entire group belongs
to the later years of his life, for none can be dated earlier
than 438 B.C. . . .

The plays are not of equal merit. Among those that have
been most highly regarded by modern critics are the *Bacchae,* a strange tale of orgiastic religious rites centered about
the female votaries of Bacchus [or Dionysus], the *Medea,*
with its theme of jealousy and revenge, the *Hippolytus,* a
story of unrequited love and deception, the *Trojan Women,* a
powerful drama of the suffering of the innocent in war, the
Iphigeneia among the Taurians, a play of adventure and escape verging on melodrama; the *Alcestis,* a tragicomedy, and
the *Electra,* with its treatment of matricide. . . .

Although Euripides was too much the detached philosopher to allow external events to color very markedly the
mythological theme of his plots, it is nonetheless interesting
in looking over the dates of the plays to reflect on the political circumstances of the years in which they were produced.
The *Alcestis* was presented in 438 B.C., the same year that
Pheidias' statue of Athena Parthenos [which stood inside the
magnificent Parthenon temple] was dedicated; the *Medea,*
offered in 431 B.C., coincided with the opening of the Peloponnesian War; the *Heracleidae* belongs to 429 B.C., the year
of Pericles' death; the *Suppliant Women* to 421 B.C., the year
of the Peace of Nicias; the *Trojan Women* was offered in 415
B.C., the year that the Athenian expedition sailed to Syracuse;
and the *Electra* in 413 B.C., the year of the destruction of that
armament. Though it would be profitless to seek specific
historical themes in the plays of Euripides, he was writing as
a citizen of Athens, and it is clear that the influences of the
contemporary scene left their impress on him, for both political change and literary productivity pursued their ways
in the crowded years of the fifth century.

THE BACKGROUND OF EURIPIDES' *MEDEA*

It is difficult to find a play of Euripides that would be generally accepted as characteristic of his work, for his range of
interest and technique is wide. Nevertheless, if one must be
selected to illustrate his achievement, the *Medea* may serve
the purpose, for no play from the Euripidean collection is
more skilfully written or more powerful in its emotional effect. As with the *Œdipus Tyrannus* [or *Oedipus the King*] of
Sophocles, the essential incidents that lie behind the seg-
ment of the story that has been chosen for the drama are
embodied in the plot itself, though the audience may also be
presumed to have had some knowledge of the circumstances that brought Jason and Medea together. Jason, the
son of Æson, and rightful heir to the throne of Iolcus in
Thessaly, had been dispatched by his usurping uncle, Pelias,
to bring back the Golden Fleece from Colchis as a labor necessary to the recovery of his birthright. With fifty chosen heroes of Greece, Jason had sailed on the Argo, and at Colchis
the king, Æëtes, had promised to surrender the Golden
Fleece if Jason would slay the sleepless dragon that guarded
it and sow its teeth. This and other tasks impossible of human accomplishment Jason was able to perform with the
aid of Medea, the sorceress daughter of Æëtes, who used her
magic art to help the Greek hero, for she had fallen passion-
ately in love with him. Together they fled from Colchis, and
Medea sealed her perpetual estrangement from her childhood home by slaying her own brother. When they reached
Iolcus, Medea again put her baleful powers at the service of
her lord, and wreaked vengeance on Pelias by persuading
his daughters that she could restore him to youth by boiling
him in a cauldron with magic herbs. In the act, however, she
omitted the herbs, and Pelias was killed. Jason and Medea
now fled to Corinth, where they lived in company with their
children. At length Creon, the king of Corinth, proposed to
have Jason wed his daughter, first putting aside Medea, the
barbarian wife from Colchis. It is at this point that the play
of Euripides opens.

In the play of Euripides a prologue was frequently used to
acquaint the audience with the setting. In the present instance
the old Nurse of Medea appears at the outset and sorrowfully
soliloquizes on the evil pass to which they have come:

Would that the Argo had never sailed to the land of the

Colchians through the dark Symplegades, and would that never in the glades of Pelion had the tall pine been felled to furnish oars for the hands of the Argonauts, who brought back with them the Golden Fleece to Pelias; for then never would my mistress Medea have sailed to the citadels of Iolcus, smitten at the heart with the love of Jason.

The further soliloquy of the Nurse, her dialogue with the attendant, and the anguished voice of Medea heard from within the palace disclose not only the imminent betrayal that Jason has resolved to commit, but also reveal the frenzy of grief and reproach into which Medea has fallen, and the wild untamed spirit of the woman, whose passion for vengeance is to form the theme of the tragedy.

MEDEA'S REVENGE

As Medea enters into the action of the play, two elements in her character and situation emerge into clear relief. One is the overmastering passion for revenge against those who have brought her to dishonor and disgrace, in which the righteous wrath of a woman mingles with the more than human frenzy of the Colchian sorceress. The second is the sense of isolation and hopelessness in which the unhappy Medea finds herself, with all sanctuary denied her, whether in her ancient home of Colchis, in Jason's former home at Iolcus, or even in humble obscurity in Corinth, for Creon, the king, requires her instant banishment. Thus we hear from the lips of Medea such words as these addressed to the Chorus of Corinthian women:

> They say that we women live a life untroubled in our homes, while men must strive with the spear. How fond is their thought! I would rather take my stand three times behind the shield in war than bear one child. But these words mean less to thee than to me, for thou hast still a city, a father's home, the joy of life, and the comradeship of friends, while I, alone and cityless, am reviled of my husband, seized captive from a foreign land. Neither mother nor brother nor kinsman have I with whom to take shelter in my misfortune. Therefore I crave one thing only from thee, that thou keep silence if any way or device be found for me to take vengeance on my husband and requite him for these ills. . . .

Medea is now resolved to act. . . . From the credulous Creon, who has ordered her banishment, she obtains a day's respite, ostensibly to prepare for her departure but in reality to make ready the fearful vengeance that shall embrace Jason, Creon, and the princess whom Jason is to marry, and which shall even encompass the death of her own sons in her obsession for revenge.

Two principal scenes take place between Jason and Medea, prior to the last exultant moment when she vaunts over him in the success of her baleful plan. The first involves a fierce quarrel, in which the . . . justification that Jason offers for his conduct is met with the withering fury of Medea's rage and scorn. . . .

The second meeting occurs when Medea has been able to carry her plans further, and in particular after she has gained from Ægeus, the king of Athens, a sworn pledge of sanctuary in his land, for it is a necessary part of her vengeance that she should live to gloat on the suffering that she has wrought, and that she should not perish in the holocaust. Hence Medea greets Jason with the pretence of reconciliation. She craves pardon for her violent words and commends the wisdom of his conduct. She would have her children remain in Corinth and live in harmony with the king. And she, too, will aid the entreaty that banishment may not be pronounced against them, for she will send by their hands gifts to the princess, Jason's new wife, a fair robe and an embossed gold chaplet. . . .

The dramatic irony of the moment brings tension, for only the sorceress knows the baneful power of her gifts. . . . Presently a messenger rushes in with the fearful news of the agonized death of the princess and her father, who have been consumed by the magic burning power of the gifts that Medea had sent. And now with cold, unnatural calm, Medea turns to the last task that confronts her, the slaughter of her own children, that Jason, too, may suffer. . . .

> I am resolved upon this deed, to slay at once my sons and quit this land, nor shall I delay that they may meet death at another and less kindly hand. For it is inevitable that they should die.

In keeping with Greek convention, the death of the children is accomplished behind the scenes, and the play closes with the arrival of Jason just in time to see his wife borne off in a chariot drawn by winged dragons, taking with her the bodies of his sons, which, with a last refinement of torture, she refuses to give up for burial. The supernatural means adopted for the conclusion of the plot illustrates the *deus ex machina*, or "the god from a machine," which was adopted with increasing frequency in the later days of Greek drama.

THE ELEMENT OF TERROR

The *Medea* is a play of powerful emotion, with bold and striking delineation of character and with a well-conceived and well-executed plot. The introduction of the *deus ex machina* [appearance of a god to resolve the plot], which ordinarily means the substitution of an inartistic convention for skilful resolution of the plot, is more acceptable in this instance because the method of its incorporation harmonizes with the magical powers of Medea herself. If the play is assessed with Aristotle's definition of tragedy in mind, it will be apparent that the element of terror rather than pity predominates in the major characters, and the cartharsis of the emotions will be sought in the spent fury of the hatred and vengeance of a woman who has been drawn as a barbarian sorceress beyond the pale of Hellenic [Greek] conduct and who therefore reveals the emotions of jealousy and revenge writ large. Where pity can be identified in the drama it will be seen in connection with the king of Corinth, his daughter, and the slain children of Jason and Medea. Nor should one fail to note the sympathy that is aroused for Medea herself as a homeless outcast even in the minds of those who must condemn the enormity of her conduct.

The long and brilliant success of this tragedy, revived in America in recent years . . . testifies to the universal principles involved, for even audiences quite untrained in Greek dramatic techniques have fallen under the spell of the tale.

EURIPIDES' SYMPATHY FOR HUMAN SUFFERING

The analysis of a single play of Euripides affords a less satisfactory understanding of the quality of his art than does a similar brief treatment of the work of Æschylus or Sophocles. This is due not only to the fact that more than twice as many tragedies of Euripides have survived as of either of the two older dramatists, but also to the wider range of interest that engaged his attention. The atmosphere of the middle of the fifth century, which led Sophocles, in common with [the great sculptors] Pheidias and Polycleitus, to create eternal and static types, was already yielding to the more personal and individualistic attitude that is to be observed in the achievements of the fourth century, and Euripides was enough younger than Sophocles to come more directly under the influence of this change of emphasis.

Hence one will not seek consistency of treatment in the various plays of Euripides, but rather he will observe the variety of emotional themes. Thus, the strained and harsh qualities of hate and vengeance that are part of the strength of the *Medea* are balanced by the softer and more tender moods of some of his other tragedies. For example, the unusually beautiful *Alcestis* tells of the love and devotion of the young queen of Thessaly, Alcestis, who gave her own life to save her husband, Admetus, when he was doomed to die if he could not find a willing substitute. The strange conduct of the boisterous, hard-drinking, but good-hearted Heracles, who enters the house of mourning unawares and presently rescues Alcestis from Death, indicates the degree to which Euripides was prepared to depart from the usual conventions of Greek tragedy.

Problems of human suffering were treated with great sympathy by Euripides. The *Trojan Women* deals, in a spirit of unrelieved sadness, with the pitiable plight of the aged queen Hecuba and the daughters of Priam after the fall of Troy and with the fate of the young Astyanax, Hector's son, who was thrown from the battlements. The verses of this tragedy carry one back to the scenes of sorrow in the *Iliad*, when Hector, parting from Andromache, foretells her lot of slavery, and when the unhappy Priam laments the sad fate of the city which must come to pass with the death of Hector.

The tense and complicated plot was masterfully handled by Euripides, and he frequently resorted to the *deus ex machina* for its solution. Such a play is the *Iphigeneia in Tauris*, which he based on a variation of the tale of the sacrifice of Iphigeneia. In the alternate legend, Artemis rescued the maid from the altar and made her priestess at a temple among the barbarous Taurians, where it was her duty to prepare for sacrifice all strangers who came to those inhospitable shores. The action of the play deals with the arrival of Orestes and Pylades, their capture, and the preparation for the sacrifice of Orestes by his sister, who knows not his identity. It thus affords admirable opportunities for Euripides to develop dramatic suspense and at length to effect with consummate skill an *anagnorisis*, or recognition scene, which resolves the story in romantic success rather than in tragedy. The happy ending of this play, as with the *Alcestis*, indicates the departure of Euripides from the more formal canons of tragic composition. . . .

EURIPIDES' MODERN QUALITIES

The kinship of Euripides with modern society has been the subject of frequent comment. It will be realized on reflection that his modernity, like the freshness of all Greek thought, lies not in any superficial resemblance to a transitory experience of present-day life, but in the universality of his themes. Thus such a theme as the devotion of Alcestis to her husband is reenacted in every instance of supreme love and sacrifice. The tenseness of the recognition in the *Iphigeneia in Tauris* depends on the same agonizing suspense that has vivified many subsequent plays; and the depths of anguish in which the wanderers from captive Troy are enveloped in the *Trojan Women* has its modern counterpart in every tale of poignant human suffering that has accompanied the devastation and exile occasioned by war in our own day.

CHAPTER 3

Greek Comedy

Greek Drama

Comedy's Origins and Early Masters

T.A. Sinclair

The origins of Greek Old Comedy are obscure, as explained in this informative essay by T.A. Sinclair, a former classicist at the University of London. After summarizing the conjectured sources of comedy (Dionysian ritual and various informal skits), Sinclair mentions some of the early comic playwrights, whose works have not survived but which are mentioned by Aristophanes and other ancient writers. Sinclair also explains the basic elements of the Old Comedy's loose structure.

The origins of Comedy are almost as obscure as those of tragedy, with which it was closely connected, but it seems certain that they are partly Dorian and partly native Attic. As early as the sixth century B.C. scenes both of mythological burlesque and of everyday life were performed at Megara on the Isthmus [of Corinth, the land bridge connecting central and southern Greece] and in the early fifth century at Megara Hyblaea and Syracuse in Sicily. The composition of these farcical sketches was associated particularly with the name of Epicharmus, who accordingly passed as the originator of comedy; but actually the work of Epicharmus, from what we know about it, was not *comodia*. The words *comodos, comodia* are connected with *comos* "revel" and *comazein*. Now there were many ways in Attica and elsewhere of *comazein* "celebrating"; a *comos* might be a serenade *en masse*, a demonstration outside someone's house or in honour of a god, especially Dionysus; it might be a phallic procession [a fertility ritual in which the worshipers carried representations of male genitalia], its members might dress as animals for some half-forgotten religious reason or for the mere pleasure of dressing up. They were, as Aristotle

Excerpted from T.A. Sinclair, *A History of Classical Greek Literature from Homer to Aristotle*. Reprinted by permission of the publisher, Routledge.

says, volunteers, who took part because they enjoyed it; but someone, we know not who, began to organize bands of revellers and train them for the Dionysiac festivals. Herein lies the Attic contribution to comedy—a trained chorus of *comodoi*. How or when this choral element was combined with the more dramatic and more narrative elements of Dorian origin we do not know, but traces of both are visible in the fully-fledged comedy of Aristophanes. The *parabasis*, that part of a play in which the chorus directly addresses the audience, is a relic of the *comos*, while the farcical interludes and probably the *agon*, or contest, may be regarded as Dorian elements.

THE EARLY COMIC PLAYWRIGHTS

The history of the development of the Old Comedy is more than obscure. Even Aristotle has to say "Who first added masks, prologues, number of actors and so forth is not known" (*Poet., v.* 3). On the purely literary side however we can readily see that just as tragedy owed much to Epic and Lyric, so parts of comedy have affinities with Iambic and Satiric verse. It was some time before Comedy received official recognition within the city of Athens—not until it had become well established in the country districts, but by the time of the Persian wars plays were being regularly performed. The prejudice however died hard, or rather it never died, but found fresh cause and lived. For there must have been a powerful section of Athenian citizens who disapproved of comedy, not because of its obscenities but because it . . . ridiculed living men. In 440 they succeeded in prohibiting this freedom. The ban was removed three years later but was reimposed in 416.

The earliest comic poets at Athens were Chionides and Magnes who were writing in the years that followed the battle of Salamis (480). Magnes, we know from Aristophanes, lived too long; his early brilliance did not last in his old age. More important is Cratinus, who flourished between 453 and 423. It was he who introduced political satire into comedy. A follower of Cimon . . . he is against the Sophists [teachers] in music and morals and against foreigners in everything. His attacks were marked by a fund of inventiveness and a torrential flow of language, and he was the main reason for the ban of 440. Cratinus' best-known play, however, is not a direct political attack. The *Dionysalexandrus* is a play of mythological burlesque, which may still have had a political application. The story of the judgment of Paris (Alexander) is retold with variations and with the god Dionysus as the central figure. Hera offers him Power, Athene success in war and Aphrodite irresistible charm for women. He chooses Aphrodite and is thus able to win Helen and induce her to leave Sparta with him. In the end, however, she passes into the hands of Paris as in the original legend. This Argument shows elaboration of plot but does not suggest that there could have been much scope for the bitter invective for which Cratinus was famous and which marked him as the literary heir of Archilochus. It is therefore likely that it belongs to a late period of Cratinus' career, when he came under the influence of the school of Crates who made more use of plot and of imaginary persons.

Very different are Crates and Pherecrates. Of the former Aristophanes speaks highly for his refinement and neat wit. He was not a political satirist but a forerunner of the urbane comedy of manners of the next century. Pherecrates was of the same nonpolitical school. In one fragment of 25 lines Pherecrates deplores the decay of flute music, blaming among others Timotheus of Miletus. There was a host of writers contemporary with Aristophanes of whom the chief are Eupolis, Phrynichus and Plato (Comicus). Eupolis, who with Cratinus and Aristophanes makes the trio of great masters of Attic comedy, was killed in the war at the age of 35. At first a friend of Aristophanes, whom he assisted in the composition of the *Knights* in 424, he afterwards quarrelled with him. The fragments of Eupolis are just long enough and numerous enough to make us wish that some of his plays had survived entire, that we might set him alongside Aristophanes. He attacks the Sophists, of course, calling Socrates "an idle penniless chatterer who had wit for everything but to earn an honest living." In his *Demes* (c. 417) he praised the eloquence of Pericles and deplored the lack of the good generals of the olden times.

TRANSPORTED TO A DIFFERENT WORLD

In comedy even more than in tragedy we must not be led astray by our use of the same word in modern times. The Old or Fifth-century Comedy differs entirely from its modern counterpart, which . . . has more affinities with Euripides. The Old Comedy honoured Dionysus in very fact; the characters are in a sense drunk, not reeling or stupefied but stimulated and inspired to do and say quite unreasonable and unaccountable things. At one moment they will delight in obscene jokes and knockabout fun, in the next they will utter high moral sentiments and even rise to pure poetry. Only Dionysus can make that possible. It becomes easy and natural to make a city midway between the heavens and earth, to converse with dead poets or living clouds. It is not that we are transported into a different world as in the fairy-tale plays of Euripides. We are in our own world but we see it through impish spectacles which sometimes distort, sometimes magnify, are sometimes highly coloured but occasionally plain. Little wonder that Old Comedy is difficult to appreciate. We cannot always tell what the players are actually doing. Without notes and references many of the jokes are meaningless. Aristophanes is always parodying tragedy; often we do not possess the original and except in a general way the force of the parody is lost. When prominent persons like Socrates or Cleon appear, we can enjoy the ridicule, but names which were well known to the audience have to be sought out by us in works of reference, perhaps only to find that nothing is known of the man beyond what is said in the passage we are reading. Yet no one who reads Aristophanes can fail to be attracted, whether by the interesting sidelights on Athenian history and Athenian character, or by the witty and acute criticism of contemporary thought, morality and literature, or by the sheer exuberant fun and the salutary occupation of being reminded that our bodily functions play a more important part in our lives than our respectability will allow us to admit.

COMEDY'S LOOSE STRUCTURE

The language of Comedy is, as one would expect, more homely and more flexible than that of tragedy; it is full of puns and of comic words coined for the occasion. When it is solemn and pompous, as it frequently is, it is generally a piece of parody. There is greater variety of rhythm and metre and the comparatively regular structure of tragedy . . . is not found in comedy. This is due partly to its complex origin; the parts of comedy are less clearly defined and it is impossible to fit them all into a single regular framework. The especial features of the Old Comedy are the *Agon* or Contest, sometimes between two actors, sometimes between two halves of the chorus or between actor and chorus; for the chorus, far from being a moderating influence as in tragedy, generally stirs up trouble and adds to the fun: and the *Parabasis* where the chorus address the audience, often in the name of the author. The parabasis itself may be divided into different parts but only a few plays have a parabasis that is complete in every detail. In Aristophanes' early period (before 420) the parabasis is generally fairly complete; the plays of second period *(Frogs, Lysistrata)* have a less perfect parabasis, while those of the third period have none at all. The concluding scene of comedy is often some kind of feast. The traditional elements in the structure of Old Comedy were thus decreasing in importance. In other matters Aristophanes himself claims to have improved comedy, to have made it more refined and intellectual, less dependent for success on mere vulgarity and horse-play or prurient suggestion:

> "No, he kept his purpose pure and high,
> That never the Muse, whom he loved to use, the villainous
> trade of the bawd should ply."

Aristophanes: Master Humorist and Social Critic

Moses Hadas

This analysis of Aristophanes' style, works, and significance is by the noted scholar and translator of ancient literature—Moses Hadas (editor of a widely-used translation of the playwright's complete surviving works). Hadas explains what made Aristophanes a great comic playwright and discusses his wit and outrageous humor, the form of the Old Comedy framework in which he labored, the comic business his actors engaged in, and his use of social satire to criticize the leading citizens of his day. In particular, says Hadas, Aristophanes attacked the sophists, who rose to prominence in the late fifth century B.C. Professional teachers who specialized in argumentation, often without taking a firm stand either way, they were roundly criticized by intellectuals, including Plato and Aristotle.

Aristophanes is not the most profound or exalted of Greek poets, but he is the most creative. Others deal with the world as it is, glorifying it, perhaps, or justifying its flaws, discovering hidden values in it and suggesting how they may be realized; Aristophanes erases the world that is and constructs another. The tragedies we have are all based on traditional myths which the playwrights might interpret and embellish—provided the embellishment were appropriate and probable—but they could not significantly alter the ancient "history." Aristophanes abolishes history and all ordinary constraints of space and time, of gravity and physiology. If war has become tiresome he makes a private treaty with the enemy or goes to heaven to fetch down the goddess Peace. If Athens has become tiresome he builds a new city in the sky.

If living poets are inadequate he goes to hell to fetch back an old one.

For their principal dramatic personae [cast of characters] the tragic poets were limited to the traditional personages of myth. If Aristophanes wants a character he invents one. To us this does not seem remarkable, but we must remember that not only epic and tragedy and choral lyric but even the dialogues of Plato used only personages who were believed to be historical. And if characters are invented so are their doings. Aristophanes created his own world, and populated it with his own people, as a god might do.

THE UNIVERSALITY OF THE COMIC

And yet these invented people behave in ways consonant with our conceptions of human nature. Once we grant the validity of the new world which Aristophanes has created, what his people do in it seems perfectly normal. This involves another important difference between comedy and tragedy. The personages of tragedy do indeed grieve and rejoice as men everywhere and always have done, else their stories would be unprofitable and indeed meaningless to us. But sometimes we need to learn a particular code to understand that causes apparently inconsequential can generate intense emotional responses. Sometimes, similarly, we need to know a particular set of conventions to recognize that a thing is incongruous and therefore funny; but the incongruities which comedy invents are seldom so subtle as to require commentary. Laughter is more direct and more universal than the emotions of tragedy.

No Athenian of the fifth century B.C. (or indeed of any other) ever saw an Agamemnon or a Clytemnestra in the flesh; these stalking figures were deliberately built up by the poets, and their costumes and mode of speech, like their emotional intensity, were calculated to set them apart from ordinary humanity. The figures of comedy, historical (like Euripides or Plato) or invented, are familiar contemporary types, and their behavior is according to familiar norms. The figures of tragedy are sometimes little more than symbols to illustrate some permanent principle of morality; those of comedy have to do with simpler but more immediate problems of making peace, running a school, writing a play. In comedy alone do men drop the rigid poses they are given in graver kinds of writing and walk and talk on a level with their fellow citizens. When the tyrant of Syracuse asked how he could discover what Athenians were like, Plato advised him to read the comedies of Aristophanes.

Aristophanes should then be the most accessible of the fifth century dramatists, and at many levels he is. He is not at all levels because preoccupation with the timely militates against timelessness. The tragic poets who deal with eternal problems write as if they knew they were addressing the ages. Aristophanes wrote for a specific audience and occasion, and would have laughed at the thought that remote generations might be fingering his plays. At the level of physiological jokes, therefore, and those that approach the physiological in universality, all who share our common physiology can understand him well enough. But allusions to contemporary persons, events, or usages, special connotations of words, and, in a more general view, the intellectual bent of Aristophanic wit sometimes leaves us in the dark—just as reflections of contemporary life in our comedy would be lost on a Greek audience. An old movie has Groucho Marx's secretary say, when two men are waiting to see him, "Epstein is waxing wroth," and Groucho replies, "Tell Roth to wax Epstein." How many volumes of commentary would a Greek require to understand all of the joke, and how unfunny it would be after he had studied the commentary! We do have helpful information to solve some puzzles in the compilations of scholia made in later antiquity, but much must remain only partially understood. But as in all classical literature so in Aristophanes also the specific merges with the general. From Aristophanes' contemporary Thucydides, for example, we learn the details of a particular war but we learn also about the nature of war generally. So in Aristophanes, if the details are not always clear the general principles are not only clear but instructive.

More basic than the difficulty of forgotten allusions is the fact that Aristophanic comedy is intellectual rather than sentimental. What the essential nature of the comic is, is still an open question, but for assaying individual creators of comedy it is convenient and it may be instructive to distinguish between the sentimental kind, which engages the reader's sympathy for its personages as human beings, and the intellectual kind, which attacks the reader's head rather than his heart, or, if we may give the words these particular meanings, between humor and wit. . . . If, in Aristophanes' *Clouds,* we feel kindly toward Socrates or Strepsiades, it is because we know Socrates from other sources and because we are sorry for old men we know who are bedeviled by wastrel sons; Aristophanes does nothing to waken our sympathy or play upon it. It is just where kindliness might be expected that we find him most heartless. He is notably cruel to old women, for example, as all writers of intellectual comedy tend to be. . . .

Intellectual fun, needless to say, is not necessarily lofty. Pie-throwing and prat-falls are intellectual jokes, not humor. The basis of the intellectual joke is manifest incongruity [an extreme lack of logic and propriety]. Very often . . . the incongruity depends on kinds of word play: a pun is funny because it brings together two meanings of a word that are really incongruous. But puns are not the only kind of incongruity. It is incongruity, not sympathy for an impoverished gentleman, that makes us laugh at a top-hat that is dented or worn with patched shoes. If it were habitual with us to keep the queer members which flap at either side of our heads scrupulously swathed, nothing could be funnier than to see them unexpectedly exposed. That is why the phalluses [penises] and talk about them which are ordinarily discreetly covered are funny when exposed to an audience.

To use Aristophanes as a stick with which to belabor the Victorians [meant here as conservative, proper people] and their progeny is false, for the Greeks too were Victorian; if they had not been, Aristophanes' bawdry would not have been incongruous and would not have amused the Greeks any more than it would have amused us. It is true that we are more reserved in these matters than were the Greeks, and hence the bawdry is to us more obtrusive; that is how "Aristophanic" has acquired its meaning. It is of course true that Aristophanes' plays are saturated with obscenity; excretory and sexual functions are explicit or implicit on every page, and dozens of seemingly innocent words apparently carried obscene connotations. But what should interest us is not that Aristophanes is so outspoken but that the rest of Greek literature is so pure, not that men seemed to relish obscenity (when have they not?) but that it was presented under the highest auspices of the state, to the entire population, at a religious festival under the presidency of a priest and on consecrated ground.

Obscenity was incongruous because Greek literature aside from comedy is one of the most decorous [proper] we know; it is more decorous, for example, than the literature of the Old Testament. It is as if dumping all bawdiness into one form served to keep the others pure, and that indeed is one implication of Euripides' *Bacchae.* The ferment which a man must exert himself to suppress if he would keep all the days of the year pure will nevertheless creep in to taint all 365 of them; but if he gives the ferment three days of carnival in which to boil itself away then he might hope to keep the other 362 untainted. The god who proved this arithmetic upon Pentheus in the *Bacchae* was of course the same Dionysus who was celebrated in the dramatic festivals.

If comedy is a wholesome purge we can understand how the enlightened authorities of a state might tolerate it, but the religious auspices must still seem odd to communicants of more austere religions. The explanation is that, as in the Greek art forms, a usage which originally had a religious rationale obvious to all came to be retained for aesthetic or other reasons after the religious burden had faded or disappeared. About the early history of comedy we know little— mainly because Aristotle did not like comedy and scanted it in his *Poetics* [in which he discussed tragedy in detail]—but there can be no doubt that its origins are to be connected with a fertility cult, in which the element of sex would naturally be central. The beast mummery [dressing in animal costumes] (as in the fantastic costuming and titles of the choruses) and the festive topsy-turvydom which gave inferiors license to make butts of their betters are surely integral to the cultic origins of comedy also. To what degree fifth-century audiences were conscious of the original significances of these elements of comedy we cannot be sure; but the sense of ritual surely remained, for the Greeks were extremely conservative in preserving established forms. Aristotle says that when an art form reaches its proper development it remains fixed. Euripides might revolutionize the spirit of tragedy, but he retained its form virtually unchanged.

It is because of its religious origins and associations, doubtless, and because Greek art is always observant of form that Aristophanes' plays fall into a regular pattern; the pattern is not so strict as tragedy's, but much more regular than in modern comedy. As in tragedy there is a *prologue;* the *parodos,* or entry of the chorus; the equivalent of *episodes,* separated from one another by fixed choral elements; and an *exodos,* or marching-away song. The chorus (usually numbering twenty-four) is much larger than the chorus of tragedy, and its apparently capricious arrangements accord to a strict pattern. In the *parabasis* the chorus comes forward to speak for the author in his own person. Here the author may justify his own work, defend himself against rivals or attack them, and here he may comment, like a columnist in a modern newspaper, on whatever abuses in the contemporary scene he may wish to animadvert upon [criticize]. It is from the parabasis of Old Comedy that the Roman genre of satire derived. At one point in the play the chorus divides into two, each half defending some point of view and abusing the other half, not only with words but sometimes even physically. Rowdy and uproarious as it may be, this contest or *agon* is usually a serious presentation of some contemporary problem. For each of the parts of the choral performance there was a prescribed meter; for example a patter song, called *pnigos* or "choker," was sung rapidly without drawing new breath.

The masks of comic actors, unlike those of tragedy, showed exaggeratedly coarse peasant types. The theory that there were a fixed set of masks—Old Man, Cook, Courtesan, etc. . . . does not apply to Old Comedy. Not only were the features of the masks coarse, but the actors were ridiculously padded on belly and buttocks, and had oversize phalluses appended. The padding allowed for all kinds of farcical business, as in the singeing of Mnesilochus in the *Thesmophoriazusae.* The prominent phalluses and the beast costumes of the chorus, as has been suggested, derived from early ritual associations of fertility cults. Providing the fanciful costumes for the chorus and training them in their intricate performances involved great expense; that is why the choral work is curtailed in Aristophanes' last plays, presented when Athens was impoverished.

The movement of an Aristophanic play is as regular as its form. The prologue, frequently a master-slave conversation, sets forth some fantastic scheme—a descent to hell, a sex strike, or the like—and the rest of the play is worked out on the assumption that the premises are the most commonplace in the world. In the agon the "good" side naturally wins and the bad is discomfited. The bad side goes off, often literally bruised, and the good goes to a riotous celebration, often accompanied by gay females. This is surely a relic of some sort of ritual "marriage" which was the culmination of a fertility celebration; psychologically it is the only accept-able solution of a comedy. The endings of tragedy, however grim they may be, are psychologically satisfying, but how else is a comedy to end?

THE TEACHING BRIEF

Aside from its creative fantasy and its purgative wit, what makes the comedy of Aristophanes memorable is its exquis-ite lyrics and its serious commentary—on politics, poetry, ed-ucation, good citizenship. The qualities of lyric poetry are no-toriously hard to communicate, in translation or description; all that can be said of Aristophanes' is that they are singularly graceful, with a sweetness that is more appealing because of the soil out of which they grow. Richest of all in this kind is the *Birds*, which the lyrics transform into an idyllic fairyland, but there are fine pieces in all the comedies. It is Aristopha-nes' lyricism, indeed, which lends his comedies wings, and that is why prose or inept verse translation is peculiarly un-fortunate in his case. Without the lift of poetry much of his terrain is a malodorous and heavy bog in which people of certain tastes may take pleasure in wallowing, but which is a travesty of Aristophanes' scintillating [sparkling] artistry.

What is more surprising than lyricism or bawdiness to innocent readers who expect of farce only that it be rollick-ing is Aristophanes' mature commentary on perennial prob-lems of political and social life. All the classic poets were looked upon and looked upon themselves as serious teach-ers . . . but none seems so conscious of a teaching mission as Aristophanes. For one thing his teaching was more explicit and immediate. The tragic poet might explore large ques-tions of the ways of God to man; the comic poet told his au-diences what was wrong with foreign policy or politicians, or how educationists were corrupting sound learning or neoteric [modern] poets corrupting good taste, and he in-vited immediate action, not merely a change in attitude. Out-spoken criticism of what Euripides called "the statues in the market place" was a carnival privilege which probably orig-inated in the revels of the fertility cult, but it has always been an element in serious comedy. . . .

So pervasive is the didactic [instructive] in Aristophanes and so consistent the tenor of his criticism that many have thought that advocacy of a particular set of doctrines was his prime object and that he chose comedy as their most effective vehicle, and some have thought that he was actually in the pay of the conservative oligarchy. Nothing could be more mistaken. The proper description of Aristophanes is poet and comic genius. His object in writing plays was to amuse, and to do it so well that he would win the prize. But an intelligent man who is funny must be funny about something, and the traditions of the form in which Aristophanes worked involved comment on matters of public interest. In this respect the comic poet was something like a newspaper columnist, and as in the case of thoughtful columnists it happened that Aristophanes' comments on all questions followed a consistent direction.

ARISTOPHANES' BELIEFS, LIKES, AND DISLIKES

The direction is at all points conservative. Aristophanes plainly does not like the relaxation of traditional standards which attended the rise of democratic power and looks back wistfully to the soberer ways of an earlier day. Like many upper-class Athenians he admired the Spartans and thought the war against them a regrettable mistake. This feeling is more or less under the surface in all the plays of the war period, but it is outspoken in the *Acharnians* and especially in the *Knights*. In the latter play he brushes aside the stunning victory of the Athenians at Sphacteria and exaggerates a minor success won by the knights at Corinth. He loathes Cleon (who took credit for the victory at Sphacteria), and thinks (in the *Wasps*) that the innovation of pay for jury duty, actually a measure to provide sustenance for the beleaguered and unemployed Athenians, was introduced by Cleon to strengthen his hold on the populace. And yet, as the *Lysistrata* shows, he is more moved by sympathy for the innocent sufferers of war than by anger against the warmongers. The amazing thing is that plays attacking the war policy when the state was at war could be given under state auspices and that Cleon could be . . . attacked for bad morals and manners when he was himself in the audience.

Aristophanes is most bitter against the sophists. . . . In order to give force to his attack on the sophists he is willing to make Socrates, who was himself opposed to the sophists, a butt, because Socrates was a familiar figure and his appearance and manner invited ridicule. This does not mean, of course, that Aristophanes' shrewd attacks on the relaxed discipline . . . favored by the new education are without point.

He strikes at Euripides in almost every play and makes him the chief butt of the *Frogs* and the *Thesmophoriazusae* because, following sophist doctrine, Euripides degraded tragedy from its lofty plane and vulgarized it by introducing commonplace characters and unseemly plots. And yet he pays Euripides the tacit compliment of imitating him, and for all his sympathy for Aeschylus, in the *Frog,* he pronounces some unkind truths about Aeschylus' own faults of pomposity and turgidity. And the *Thesmophoriazusae* is a delightful piece of literary playfulness, wholly without malice. He dislikes innovations in music, and thinks the old tunes were better because they fostered manly discipline. He dislikes theories of social reform pointing to socialism or communism, mainly because people cannot in nature be equal as these systems premise. Human nature, he holds, cannot be transformed by legislation. . . . He is thoroughly Athenian in making the interest of the state the gauge for all values: when Dionysus cannot decide between Euripides and Aeschylus on grounds of poetic merit (in the *Frogs*) the decision is reached by the soundness of the political advice which each offers. It is significant that the *Birds,* which is the most carefully wrought of all the plays, is also the most charming and utterly free from malice. It is the sad state of the human condition, and not a particular set of malefactors, that prompts the establishment of a utopia in a fanciful never-never land.

One final quality of the plays, which tells us more about the audience than the playwright, must be mentioned, and that is the volume of literary allusion which the audience was expected to recognize. There are allusions or intentionally garbled quotations from tragedy . . . in all the plays; the *Thesmophoriazusae* and the *Frogs* turn on quotations, mainly from Euripides, and the *Frogs* expects of its audience a high degree of sophistication in literary criticism. All of this would be understandable in works directed to an esoteric audience of scholars; but these plays were addressed to the whole population, and were meant to win prizes. . . . We have no better evidence than the plays of Aristophanes for the high level of general literary sophistication in Athens, as we have no better evidence than his plays for the effectiveness of Athenian *eleutheria* and *parrhesia,* liberty and freedom of speech.

Except for the parabases of his own plays, in which he

speaks of his own and his rivals' works, we know no more of Aristophanes than we do of the writers of tragedy. One distinction of Aristophanes is that whereas the surviving plays of Sophocles and Euripides were written in full maturity and most near the ends of their long lives, those of Aristophanes, except for the *Ecclesiazusae* and the *Plutus,* are a young man's work. Aristophanes was born about 445 B.C., and the *Acharnians,* produced in 425 when he was barely twenty, is a fully mature work. Details given in the ancient Lives are extrapolations from his plays or imaginary. His death cannot have occurred before 388 B.C.

In all, forty-four plays were attributed to Aristophanes, and of these some were produced under the names of other poets. The fact that the eleven plays of Aristophanes which we have are the only complete specimens of Old Comedy to survive is sufficient proof that his work was esteemed the best. Five of the eleven plays we have—*Acharnians, Knights, Clouds, Wasps,* and *Peace*—were produced one each year from 425 to 421. Then follow the *Birds,* Aristophanes' acknowledged masterpiece, 414; *Lysistrata* and *Thesmophoriazusae,* 411; and *Frogs,* 405. The fall of Athens in 404 was a blow to comedy as to other aspects of Attic creativity, and the two last plays of our corpus show spiritual as well as physical impoverishment. The *Ecclesiazusae,* produced in 392 B.C., shows a flagging of comic verve; the choral portions are perfunctory, and at one place our texts give merely the word "Chorus." *Plutus,* produced in 388 B.C., leaves the exuberant farce of the earlier Aristophanes almost entirely and makes a transition to the comedy of manners. There is no longer criticism of persons and policies but a travesty of the myth of the blind god of wealth to which no individual could take exception and which is applicable to any age or place. . . .

There were, of course, many other masters of Old Comedy, a number of whom defeated Aristophanes in competitions, just as there were tragic poets who defeated Aeschylus, Sophocles, or Euripides. . . . It is clear that Aristophanes towered above his rivals by a greater interval than any tragic poet above his. . . .

His influence on subsequent satire and farce is very great. But valuable as he may be as a commentary on a uniquely valuable area of human experience or as a begetter of art in others, his true claim upon our attention is as the most brilliant and artistic and thoughtful wit our world has known.

How Serious Was the Tone of Greek Comic Satire?

Stephen Halliwell

For a long time, most modern scholars held the view that Old Comedy playwrights like Aristophanes used their comic plays to launch serious attacks on those they disagreed with in an attempt to effect social change. In this view, the *parabasis,* a section in which the chorus speaks directly to the audience, reflected a playwright's actual, and quite serious opinions about some social ill. According to the opposing and now more commonly accepted view expressed here by Stephen Halliwell, a professor of Greek at the University of St. Andrews, such social satire was not nearly so serious in tone or intent. There is no evidence, says Halliwell, of major social changes or leaders dislodged from office resulting from the lampoons of comic satire.

The overwhelming impression left by Aristophanic humour is of an imaginative world that is unlimitedly zany, grotesque, and fluid. Despite this, scholars and critics have long been interested in seeking, and have often claimed to discover, a layer of seriousness in the playwright's work. While fantasy . . . is the dominant mode of Old Comedy, the materials of fantasy are of course frequently drawn, through all their distortions, from aspects of the contemporary political and social world of Athens. It is, at root, the interplay between fantasy and reality which has given rise to sharply contrasting judgements of Aristophanes' dramatic aims and character. For a long time after the Renaissance the extremes of this disagreement were posed chiefly in moral terms, with Aristophanes regarded either as a shameless, indiscriminate jester or as a moral, didactic chastiser [punisher] of reprobates [morally unprinci-

Reprinted from Aristophanes, *Birds, Lysistrata, Assembly-Women, Wealth.* A new verse translation, with an introduction and notes by Stephen Halliwell (1997), by permission of Oxford University Press. Copyright © Stephen Halliwell 1997.

pled people]. The play most often treated as a test case in this debate was *Clouds,* where the question at issue was whether Aristophanes had wantonly attacked the blameless Sokrates, or had perhaps used the figure of Sokrates as a means of exposing the subversive fraudulence of very different types of intellectuals, especially the Sophists. . . .

From the early nineteenth century, however, the focus of debate over Aristophanic satire shifted markedly towards the arena of politics. The central questions, which have tended to dominate scholarship on the playwright ever since, became: was Aristophanes a committed, purposeful satirist, in his treatment both of individual leaders and of the workings of democracy? and, if so, where did he stand in terms of the major political affiliations of late fifth-century Athens? . . . For most of the last 150 years the majority view has been that Aristophanes *was* in some degree committed to expressing political judgements in his comedies, especially through the use of satire. But there has been much less agreement about exactly what those judgements were, or from what kind of general stance they were delivered. Commonest is the inference that Aristophanes was a 'conservative', which is defined in this context principally in terms of opposition to the radical democracy of the time and a hankering after an earlier, supposedly more moderate era of Athenian politics. But there have been many variations on and modifications to this inference, with arguments being advanced for Aristophanes the 'oligarch' (opposed to democracy *per se*), Aristophanes the true democrat (opposed above all to the abuse of power by demagogues and others), Aristophanes the champion of the rural classes—and other positions besides. . . . What I shall attempt . . . is to offer some general reasons for caution about deducing Aristophanes' personal allegiances from his comedies.

THE BUTTS OF ARISTOPHANES' SATIRE

The plays of Aristophanes contain such frank and often extreme satirical elements precisely because they belong to a special genre of festival entertainment. . . . Old Comedy enjoyed a peculiar freedom, which expresses itself in obscenity as well as (and often at the same time as) satire, to break the taboos and contravene the norms which obtained in the social world at large. This freedom stemmed partly from 'folk' practices of scurrilous jesting and inebriated [drunken]

celebration of the kind which Aristophanes himself twice in-
corporates in his surviving plays. What is so telling about
this side of comedy is the 'irresponsibility' of its licence to
ridicule, to lampoon, and to vilify. The playwrights of the
genre were exempted from any need to explain or answer
for their choice of satirical targets. Unlike the personal abu-
siveness which undoubtedly played a part in political life,
comedy was not usually constrained by the possibility of legal reprisals, nor by the pressures involved in persuading an
audience to take a practical decision (other than the judges'
voting of a prize to the best comedy) on a particular occasion. These differences are culturally and psychologically
fundamental, and without them it would be impossible to
explain why classical Athens permitted comedy a type and
degree of freedom which was not available in other contexts
of public life. . . . If a comic playwright was entitled to denigrate and attack with impunity, the conditions do not exist in
which his individual attitudes can be readily identified as
such through the medium of unbridled mockery. With rare
exceptions . . . comedy was, so to speak, disconnected from
the procedures of challenge, justification, and even reprisal
which applied in the life of the polis in general.

In the case of many victims of satire, comic prominence
should be taken as a reflection not of scandalous notoriety
but of the achievement of status and power within the city.
This is most obviously true of leading politicians, generals,
and office-holders (Perikles, Kleon, Hyperbolos, Lamachos,
etc.), but while our evidence is often inadequate for certainty, we can be confident that this was true of many of the
lesser targets as well. Kleonymos, for example, is set up as a
glutton and coward in several of Aristophanes' plays, but we
know that he was politically prominent on more than one
important occasion. . . . Similarly, the Kinesias who appears
as . . . a physical freak, at *Birds* 1 372 ff. and elsewhere, was
very probably a much more significant figure, both culturally (as composer and chorus-trainer) and even politically,
than we would ever guess from a literal-minded reading of
his persona in Aristophanes. Naturally not all butts of satire
were eminent or influential, but, like many later satirists,
Aristophanes did not waste much of his humour on utter social misfits or outcasts. Aristophanic ridicule has an intrin-
sically debasing and degrading thrust, and therefore an in-
built tendency to direct itself against targets which permit a

satisfying disparity between accepted realities outside the theatre and the grotesque reductiveness [diminishment] of comedy itself. In this respect Old Comedy's mockery of human beings is parallel to its burlesque presentation of the gods. Just as most readers would not now infer Aristophanes' own religious attitudes, nor prevailing currents of religious feeling in Athens, from the treatment of Hermes in *Peace, Birds,* or *Wealth,* of Iris and Poseidon in *Birds,* or of Dionysos in *Frogs,* so we should be highly circumspect [prudent] about translating his satire of individual Athenians into a personal set of political or social convictions.

THE PURPOSE OF THE PARABASIS?

At this point we need to address a seemingly obvious objection. This amounts to the commonly stated orthodoxy that comic playwrights *did* possess, in their parabases (and occasionally elsewhere too), means of announcing to their audiences the specific points of view from which they observed the life of their polis. . . . In *Acharnians,* for example, the chorus explains that Aristophanes believes himself to have been responsible for many benefits to the democracy, especially by drawing to its attention (in his recent play *Babylonians*) the deceitful flattery of foreign ambassadors who come to address the Assembly in Athens (*Acharnians* 633 ff.). The poet, they suggest, is not afraid to speak out in the interests of justice, and thereby to serve his people as adviser and teacher (ibid. 645–58). In similar vein, the chorus of *Wasps* reports Aristophanes' boast that he has not indulged in petty ridicule of ordinary people but has deployed his satire against the biggest of targets, namely the politician Kleon, who is here allegorically described as a monster whom it requires Heraklean powers to overcome (1029–35, cf. *Peace* 751–8). Aristophanes, the chorus claims, has fought and continues to fight on behalf of the Athenian people (*Wasps* 1037).

But it is a naive error to suppose that any such passage offers us the direct or authentic voice of the poet himself. The parabasis, though always standing outside the progress of the dramatic action, is none the less a full part of the comic performance. Its elaborate formality (rhythmical, musical, and choreographic) . . . provides a highly stylized interlude which is a theatrical event in its own right. Moreover, the 'voice' of the poet which can be incorporated in a parabasis is a conventional fiction, an opportunity for comedy to bur-

lesque the postures of public discourse which were so familiar to Athenian audiences from the political Assembly,
the adversarial contests of the law courts, and other democratic institutions. When in his parabases Aristophanes
'speaks', whether in the first or third person, to the city, he
can always be seen to be engaging in a more-or-less parodic
rhetoric, an assumed role of adviser, teacher, defendant, or
the like. . . . In *Wasps* . . . Aristophanes' depiction of himself
as a quasi-Heraklean enemy of Kleon is an exercise in ex-
travagantly hyperbolical bluster, the spirit of which matches
the comically outrageous terms . . . in which Kleon is transmogrified into a physically repulsive mongrel. Finally, and
very tellingly, the boast of fighting for the people is a trans-
parently rhetorical cliche, and as such was twice satirized
earlier in the play—ironically through the mouth of Philok-
leon himself, and directly by his son—as a hallmark of slick,
exploitative orators.

THE FORCE OF COLLECTIVE LAUGHTER

In short, there is nothing authoritative about anything said in
the poet's name in a parabasis, since the poet's voice is part
of, not a detached commentary on, the theatrically inflated
world of the play. Indeed, the kind of argument I have been
criticizing could profitably be stood on its head: it is the
mock-seriousness, the posturing rhetoric, and the pretence of
didactic [instructive] influence found in some parabases
which reinforce our grounds for supposing that Old Comedy
is a perpetual creator of illusions and fabrications about itself
as about everything else. As for the general issue of satirical
purpose in Aristophanes, it is practically inevitable that a
form of comedy predicated on the licence to abuse, denigrate,
and lampoon should give the *impression* of political and
other commitments. In most social contexts, forthright mockery is a weapon of aggression, superiority, or contempt. But
Athenian democracy had allowed comic drama to develop,
however riskily, as a carefully defined festive opportunity for
scurrility-without-responsibility. From at least the time of
Kratinos, in the generation before Aristophanes, poets had
exploited this opportunity to expose leading politicians, generals, and other office-holders, as well as a range of lesser individuals, to the force of collective laughter. If we ask why
this should have been so, it is impossible to avoid a culturally
and psychologically speculative model of explanation. . . .

The state festivals at which comedy, like tragedy, was performed were occasions on which the city distributed marks and awards of honour to pre-eminent citizens. They were also occasions which, even outside comic drama as such, traditionally made room for the carnivalesque pleasures of ritual mockery and licensed obscenity. It is as if the distinctively intense, heady atmosphere of Dionysiac festivals was thought simultaneously appropriate for the opposing extremes of solemn, civic earnestness and disruptive, topsy-turvy play. More interestingly still, the recipients of honorific and satirical attention were in some cases the very same people, as, for example, with the city's generals, who were granted rights of front seating (*prohedria*) in the theatre, but who might then find themselves, as Kleon and others did, the object of vilification in the very plays they were watching. Satirical mockery may, in a psychologically subtle way, have temporarily counterbalanced and inverted the possession of public power or esteem, but it is hard to believe that it could have been allowed to negate or cancel out these things. And indeed our evidence is not, in my view, encouraging to a belief in comedy's potency as an influence upon currents of publicity or public opinion in classical Athens. The famous case of Plato's *Apology*, with its references to Sokrates' treatment in the *Clouds* (18c–19c), has been overworked in this respect. It is far from clear that Plato ascribes real influence to the comedy in dissemination of a false picture of the philosopher's interests; more likely he is citing *Clouds* as a pointed illustration of just how ludicrous the distortions of Sokrates' life could become. Be that as it may, Plato was not actually well placed, still less sufficiently impartial, to be a precise witness of the effect of *Clouds* (a play which flopped, it seems, at its first performance) on Athenian views of Sokrates. In the case of Kleon, Aristophanes' own parabatic boast of having floored the politician, as in a wrestling contest (*Clouds* 549–50), is a self-evident piece of pseudo-political arrogance: if anything, Kleon's power and prestige in Athens grew greater during the very years when Aristophanes was lampooning him in often scabrous style.

No Deep Insights

Because comic performances were limited to two main festivals in the year, they were not sufficiently embedded in the all-year-round processes of social and political life to make any regular or much practical difference to them. This is not to say that comedy was 'innocent fun'. Its unfettered freedom of speech permitted it to voice feelings of dissatisfaction, exasperation, irreverence, and cynicism which no doubt partially reflected the underside of political consciousness in the city. But we will be prone to considerable self-deception if we think that we now have much chance of picking our way through its distortions, its absurdities, its contradictions, and its outrageous transformations of life, and coming out at the end with a coherent or steady sense of the playwright's own point of view. All humour tends to some extent towards the dissolution of sense, and the characteristic modes of Old Comedy do so to an exceptional degree. Aristophanes' theatrical strength lies in the fertility of his inventiveness and the multifariousness [versatility] of his talent for manipulating images and ideas into surprising yet satisfying scenarios. But anyone who looks to him for deep insights into Athenian society is likely to be ultimately disappointed.

Euripides' *Cyclops*: The Only Complete Surviving Satyr-Play

David Grene and Richmond Lattimore

Satyr-plays were not comedies in the strict sense, since they were staged as part of the tragic, rather than the comedic, presentations at the City Dionysia. However, though the underlying themes and morals of satyr-plays were usually of a serious nature, their plots and overall tone were invariably absurd and meant to make audiences laugh. Typically, they featured obscene humor, both visual and verbal, performed in part by satyrs (half-man, half-animal), with the mythical horse-man, Silenus, frequently a leading character. This informative commentary on Euripides' *Cyclops*, the only existing complete satyr-play (part of one of Sophocles' satyr-plays has also survived), is by the renowned scholar-translators David Grene and Richmond Lattimore.

Interest in Euripides' *Cyclops* is generally justified historically: other than a chunk of Sophocles' *Ichneutae*, it is the only example of a satyr-play, that ribald piece which in the dramatic festivals crowned a group of three tragedies or a tragic trilogy. But the *Cyclops* is more than historically interesting; it is, by modern standards, good fast farce, clearly stageworthy, with a fine dramatic intelligence behind it. The movement is typically Euripidean, not merely in the sharp reversal of roles and sympathies [and] the crisp dialogue . . . but in formal structure and underlying idea as well. Moreover, despite the play's sportive obscenity and knockabout humor, its underlying idea is essentially serious. The *Cyclops,* that is, may be clearly a farce, but it is primarily a farce of ideas, a gay and ironic flirtation with the problem of civilized brutality. As such, it lies within the main stream of

Euripides' tragic thought, and, if its treatment and tone differ from that of tragedy, the difference is less a difference of dramatic quality or genius than a difference of genre.

We should like to know a great deal more about satyr-drama as a genre than we do, and we should especially like to know what in fifth-century practice was the formal connection between a satyr-play and the three tragedies which preceded it. But unfortunately the *Cyclops* is undated and cannot, with any degree of certainty, be assigned to one of the extant [surviving] tragedies. In the absence of that crucial information, it becomes difficult to speak with assurance of the formal nature of the play or to generalize from it to the formal definition of fifth-century satyr-drama. Indeed, even if we possessed the requisite information, the very distance which separates the tragedy of Euripides from that of Aeschylus and Sophocles would tend by analogy to preclude a generalization about satyr-plays. One ancient writer, it is true, speaks of satyr-drama as being "tragedy-at-play" or "joking tragedy." But this is hardly helpful, since it may mean either that satyr-drama was mock tragedy . . . or pure farce, or simply a sportive treatment of the subject matter of tragedy. All of these are possibilities applicable to the *Cyclops*, but we have no evidence which might allow us to decide among them.

THE SATYR-PLAY'S ORIGINS AND FORM

In point of origins the satyr-play, like both comedy and tragedy, was closely bound up with Dionysiac fertility ritual. Even in the fifth-century satyr-drama in its frequent obscenity, its conventional use of Silenus as "nurse" and companion of Dionysus, and its chorus of satyrs with their *phalloi* [prominently displayed penises] preserves more vividly than tragedy the memory of its origins. What the original connection between tragedy and comedy and "satyr" may have been, we do not know, though Aristotle in a much disputed passage asserts that the satyr-play was one of the early stages of tragedy; but the value of the testimony appears doubtful. On the whole, scholars have preferred to believe that both satyr-drama and tragedy are independent developments of Dionysiac ritual. . . . Alternatively, it is held that the double aspect of Dionysiac ritual—the mourning for the dead god and the joyous celebration at his resurrection—accounts for the connection between tragedy and the satyr-play. On this theory tragedy contains the *agon* [contest] of the dying god, while the satyr-play, like comedy, exhibits the happy celebration for the reborn god and the ritual of the sacred marriage and rounds off the complete drama of the rite in a sportive coda. The presence in the *Cyclops* of an attenuated *komos* [revel] and a hinted mock (male) marriage between Silenus and Polyphemus offers some slight evidence for the theory. But it is this very attenuation of the ritual element in the play that reminds us that a theory of formal origins does not really explain what we need to know—the *literary* use and the meaning of the developed form. An account of origins may perhaps explain the conventions of a given form, but it will seldom explain the conscious literary deployment of those conventions.

For the rest our information is tantalizingly slight. Thus we know that the satyr-plays were briefer than the tragedies (the *Cyclops* is the shortest of extant plays); they had their own peculiar choral dance, the *sikinnis,* and they allowed . . . a very slight relaxation from tragic standards in the direction of colloquial speech. For its material satyr-drama drew upon the same sources in myth . . . as tragedy. Thus the *Oresteia* [by Aeschylus] appears to have been followed by the *Proteus,* a satyr-play dealing with Menelaus' Egyptian adventure with the Old Man of the Sea, while the *Cyclops* is a conflation of the Polyphemus episode from the ninth book of the Odyssey with the story of the capture of Dionysus by Lydian pirates. Both the chorus of satyrs and its "father" Silenus form a standard part of satyric convention, and their characters are accordingly stylized: the satyrs are boisterous, childlike "horse-men" (*not* "goat-men") with a strong streak of cowardice, while Silenus is at every point . . . lewd, fat, bald, drunken, boastful, knavish, and foolish. . . .

A Barbarian and a Thief

In plot and detail Euripides' adaptation of his Homeric material is remarkably close. If Odysseus here does not escape from the cave by clinging to a ram's belly, and if the immense boulder which in Homer blocked the cave has here been rolled away, these are clearly alterations demanded by the necessities of theatrical presentation. In Euripides the Cyclops is still the creature of his belly, a barking barbarian, and Odysseus is still in some sense the shrewd and civilized man who manages by exercise of mother wit to mutilate the

man-eating monster and escape. Or so, at least, it might
seem if we possessed only the first half of the play. But the
Cyclops is not merely a dramatic retelling of Homer; rather,
it is Homer's parable of the civilized man and the savage systematically anachronized into its fifth-century equivalent,
an altogether different parable.

Neither Odysseus nor Polyphemus [the Cyclops] is really

SILENUS GREETS ODYSSEUS

In these brief excerpts from the opening scene of Euripides'
Cyclops, *the leader of the satyrs, Silenus, gives the famous
warrior Odysseus the bad news that he has arrived in a land of
cannibals.*

Silenus
    I see a Greek ship drawn up on the shore
    and oarsman led by a captain coming
    toward our cave. They carry water-pitchers
    and empty containers about their necks:
    they'll want supplies. Poor strangers, who are they?
    They can't know our master Polyphemus,
    coming like this to the maneater's cave
    and looking for a welcome in his maw.
    But hush, so we can learn from where they've come,
    and why, to Sicily and Mt. Etna.

    *(Odysseus appears on the right. He carries a sword. A wine-flask
    made of skin is suspended from his neck; a cup is attached to the
    cord. He is followed by crew-members carrying pitchers and jugs.)*

Odysseus
    Strangers, could you tell us where we might find
    running water? We have nothing to drink.
    Would some one of you like to sell some food
    to hungry sailors? *What?* Do I see right?
    We must have come to the city of Bacchus [Dionysus].
    These are satyrs I see around the cave.
    Let me greet the oldest among you first.
Silenus
    Greeting, stranger. Who are you, and from where?
Odysseus
    I am Odysseus of Ithaca, king of the Cephallenians.
Silenus
    I've heard of you: a glib sharper, Sisyphus' bastard.
Odysseus
    I am he. Keep your abuse to yourself.

Homeric at all. Odysseus is not the type of the civilized man, and the Euripidean Cyclops . . . has passed directly from barbarism to decadence without pause for civilization Both manifest late fifth-century types of corruption: Odysseus' Homeric heroism in its new context is systematically undercut, less heroism than a transparent vainglory and depraved eloquence; Polyphemus is . . . an outright exponent of philo-

Silenus
From what port did you set sail for Sicily?
Odysseus
We come from Troy and from the war there.
Silenus
What? Couldn't you chart your passage home?
Odysseus
We were driven here by wind and storm.
Silenus
Too bad. I had the same misfortune. . . .
Odysseus
What is this place? Is it inhabited?
Silenus
This is Etna, the highest peak in Sicily.
Odysseus
Where are the walls and the city-towers?
Silenus
This is no city. No man inhabits here.
Odysseus
Who does inhabit it? Wild animals?
Silenus
The Cyclopes. They live in caves, not houses.
Odysseus
Who governs them? Or do the people rule?
Silenus
They are savages. There is no government. . . .
Odysseus
Are they hospitable to strangers here?
Silenus
Strangers, they say, make excellent eating.
Odysseus
What? You say they feast on human flesh?
Silenus
Here every visitor is devoured.

Quoted in David Grene and Richmond Lattimore, eds., *The Complete Greek Tragedies: Euripides, Vol. 3*. Chicago: University of Chicago Press, 1959, pp. 236–238.

sophical egoism and the immoralist equation of might and right. Euripides has taken considerable pains, moreover, to indicate to his audience that this is no longer Homer's world, but their own. Thus, when Odysseus first appears, he is greeted by Silenus as a "glib sharper" and "son of Sisyphus." Now, whatever Odysseus may be in Homer, he is never merely a "glib sharper," and his father is Laertes, not Sisyphus. To an audience bred on Homer the distinction is revealing: at one blow Euripides deprives Odysseus of his Homeric paternity in order to attach him to Sisyphus, the proverbial type of cheat and thief, and thereby warns his audience of what they may expect. Odysseus is in fact the familiar depraved politician. . . . He stands, as he almost always does in tragedy, for that refinement of intellect and eloquence which makes civilized brutality so much more terrible than mere savagery. In the *Cyclops,* however, he is on the defensive. . . . If we sympathize with Odysseus at first, this initial sympathy is nonetheless quickly alienated by the sheer . . . brutality of his revenge and by Polyphemus' transformation into a drunken, almost lovable, buffoon. The gory description of the Cyclops' cannibalism may perhaps justify Odysseus' revenge, but it does not thereby redeem its barbaric cruelty. . . . So the *Cyclops* shows, not the distinction, but the identity, between Odysseus and Polyphemus.

JUSTIFYING EMPIRE

Odysseus' speech for . . . mercy is the crux of the play. . . . It opens with a disclaimer of responsibility for the Trojan War: "A god was responsible; don't blame men." Such disclaimers in Euripides normally operate to damn those who make them, as, for instance, Helen's disavowal of responsibility in the *Trojan Women.* The next argument sounds very strange indeed. The Greeks, Odysseus argues, have preserved the temples of Poseidon (father of Cyclops) and saved Hellas [Greece]; therefore the Cyclops, who is Greek because he lives in Greek Sicily . . . should spare Odysseus and his men. What we have here is a covert but unmistakable allusion to the Persian Wars, when Athens claimed to have saved Hellas and the ancestral gods from the Persians. . . .

What Odysseus is urging here is nothing more or less than the argument which Athens had used to acquire her empire: Athens had saved Hellas and should have the rewards of her deed. This sanction for empire was employed

down to the time of the Peloponnesian War to coerce neu-
trals and unwilling states into the Athenian orbit, and the
sanction was as loathsome to most Greeks as the Athenian
Empire. Herodotus, writing in the forties [of the fifth cen-
tury], is so much aware of the unpopularity of Athens and
her sanction that he is reluctant to state the real truth which
underlies the sanction—Athens *did* save Hellas. In 432 B.C.,
just before the outbreak of the Peloponnesian War, the unof-
ficial Athenian envoys at Sparta could say of their empire:

> We have a fair claim to our possessions. . . . We need not re-
> fer to remote antiquity . . . but to the Persian War and con-
> temporary history we must refer, although we are rather
> tired of continually bringing this subject forward.

By 416, the Athenian generals at Melos could argue naked
imperialism; the empire had outgrown its sanction:

> We shall not trouble you with specious pretences . . . either of
> how we have a right to our empire because we overthrew the
> Persians, or are now attacking you because of wrong that you
> have done us . . . since you know as well as we do that right,
> as the world goes, is only in question between equals in
> power, while the strong do what they can and the weak suf-
> fer what they must.

This, then, is the sanction Odysseus urges, and it is one
whose irony it would be difficult for his audience to miss.
The irony lies in the fact that an argument normally used to
deny mercy to others is here being used to obtain it. . . . If
Odysseus speaks in part the language of the Athenian im-
perialists and in part the language of the Melians, the Cyclops outdistances him by far. Devoid of respect for the
gods, his religion is his belly and his right his desires. He
speaks . . . a straightforward egoism resting on an appeal to
Nature for the disregard of morality. *Nomos* [civilized cus-
tom], so far as he is concerned, is a mere convention of the
weak to elude the strong. In the contrast, then, of Polyphemus and Odysseus we have no Homeric contrast of barbarism and cool civilized intelligence, but a juxtaposition of
two related types of civilized brutality whose difference is
merely that of circumstance, one being weak, the other
strong. It is because neither Cyclops nor Odysseus has any
genuine moral dignity, because both of them are shown as
effectively brutal and corrupt, that the bloody blinding of
Polyphemus can come as close to pathos as it does without
becoming any less comic.

TWO BRUTAL CHARACTERS WHO DESERVE EACH OTHER

The ending is in fact superbly controlled. As usual in Euripides, the sympathy invoked for one character is suddenly alienated and shifted to another; the victim and the oppressor change places. Polyphemus, from being first a Homeric cannibal . . . is suddenly turned into a decadent, rather likable buffoon who loathes war, understands generosity, and tipsily "rapes" Silenus. Odysseus makes his bid for glory by blinding this cannibal oaf while he sleeps drunkenly. The shift in sympathy is not decisive, because no real principle is involved; but it is not therefore illusory. Odysseus' action is contemptible, but not quite criminal; Polyphemus gets what he deserves, but we pity him. That we are meant to view the action in this way seems clear both in Polyphemus' final prophecy of trouble for Odysseus and in Odysseus' statement that he would have done wrong had he burned Troy but not avenged his men. Whatever his rights in avenging his men may be, they are not sanctioned by the burning of Troy, an action which the Cyclops condemns, and with him Euripides. The truth is that Odysseus and the Cyclops deserve, not justice, but each other. The *Cyclops* in its seriousness and its humor plays about a struggle for justice between two men who either distort justice or deny its existence and who cannot therefore meaningfully claim it when wronged. And yet they get it.

The Humanity of Menander and the New Comedy

Jacqueline de Romilly

The so-called New Comedy, which developed in the late fourth century B.C., was tamer, less inventive, and far less political and obscene than the Old Comedy. In the hands of its master, Menander, however, the New Comedy entertained by exploring humane virtues such as tolerance, understanding, and forgiveness. Noted scholar Jacqueline de Romilly, formerly of the Collège de France, here summarizes Menander's works, style, characters, and humane tone.

We call "Hellenistic" the age that began with the death of Alexander in 323 [B.C.] and lasted until the beginnings of the Roman Empire. The name was designed to evoke the diffusion of Hellenism [Greek culture] into non-Greek countries and the exchanges that resulted. From the perspective of literary history, we see in this period a movement counter to the one that in the fifth and fourth centuries had drawn everything toward Athens. Menander was an Athenian, but his plays . . . were not intended for Athenian festivals only. Soon the prestige of Alexandria [in Egypt, ruled by the Greek dynasty established by Alexander's general, Ptolemy] eclipsed that of Athens. . . .

In the Hellenistic world—a world no longer bounded by the city and one in which city-states in general played an ever-diminishing role—literature became more independent of politics. New Comedy took no political stance, and rarely contained topical allusions; neither Theocritus nor Callimachus wrote political poetry; the philosophers were in search of an ethic for the individual, and said of the wise man that he "had no homeland." It would take the interest of

Excerpted from Jacqueline de Romilly, *A Short History of Greek Literature*, translated by Lillian Doherty (Chicago: University of Chicago Press). Copyright ©1985 by The University of Chicago.

the historian and, above all, the growth of a powerful new political entity—soon making itself felt even in Greece—to bring back, with Polybius, the old concern for the problems of states in general.

MENANDER'S WORKS AND STYLE

The beginning of Menander's career coincides exactly with the beginning of the Hellenistic age. Born in 342–41 B.C., he staged his first play (the *Orge*) in 321, two years after Alexander's death; he seems to have lived until 293. In his youth he . . . attended Aristotle's school, where he made the acquaintance of Theophrastus [the scholar who succeeded Aristotle as head of the school]. So he is a good representative of the spirit of the new schools. He was apparently invited to Egypt and to Macedonia, but remained in Athens. The invitations are a sign of the times, while his refusal keeps him within the Athenian tradition.

Until the beginning of the twentieth century we had only uncertain and indirect knowledge of Menander. There were fragments of his work quoted by other authors, as well as Latin imitations. . . . There were also comments and words of praise from ancient authors. Then the papyrologists began to restore Menander to us. A first series of important finds occurred in 1905. But the major discovery was that of an entire play, the *Dyskolos* (=“The Misanthrope”), published in 1959. . . . From then on, editions and commentaries multiplied; *The Samian Woman* and *The Shield* were recovered. Other finds followed: four years after the *Dyskolos,* long passages of *The Sicyonian* were published in Paris . . . then fragments of the *Misoumenos* were published in England. . . . We can probably expect more good surprises. . . . We are told that Menander wrote 108 comedies. . . .

A comedy by Menander is quite unlike the plays of the Old Comedy. The imaginative freedom is gone, as are the fixed structures within each play *(parabasis, agon,* etc.). The chorus has lost its role altogether and is reduced to providing musical interludes dividing the play into acts, or into parts that henceforth deserve that name. Each comedy includes a prologue, in the form of a long monologue (in the *Dyskolos,* it is spoken by the god Pan); this monologue, like those of Euripides, explains the sometimes complex circumstances of the action, which then unfolds from act to act. Clearly plot has become an essential element, as in the last tragedies of Euripides.

To some extent, the plots reflect the troubled times in which Menander lived: they constantly involve unidentified children, some born in the absence of a father who is on a distant voyage, some kidnaped, some abandoned and raised by the chance comer. But to Menander these upheavals merely furnish pretexts for misunderstandings he can ravel and unravel. On this basis he puts together the most complicated plots one could wish; and, like Euripides, he loves the theatrical effects of last-minute recognitions. His frequent use of courtesans [prostitutes] complicates matters further by adding jealousy to the pot, so that his imbroglios [entanglements] have still greater repercussions.

In *The Arbitrators* a young couple is separated because the wife has borne a child shortly after the wedding; the young husband is indignant, but he had raped his wife during a festival before the wedding, without knowing who she was. A harp girl he takes up with out of spite then complicates things by posing as the mother of the child. To make a long story short, there is a fine string of misunderstandings before the happy reconciliation.

In *The Shorn Girl,* a pair of abandoned twins have been entrusted to two different families. One day the brother (who has been brought up a free and rich man, and knows nothing of his past) kisses his sister (who knows everything); her hair is cut by the man she lives with, who is furiously jealous. In the end this man marries her, in an atmosphere of euphoria regained.

In *The Samian Woman,* a child is again at issue, this one born while the master of the house is away and replaced by another. All kinds of suspicions result: the master suspects his own son of having cuckolded him with the Samian woman. In fact, one child has died, and the survivor, whom the Samian has passed off as her own, is the child of the son and—the very woman who is chosen to be his wife!

Chance . . . plays a major part in all of this, and Menander does not fail to point to its omnipotence, blindness, and malice. . . . Yet the author's artistry plays an even greater role, and the constant play of misunderstandings offers him a comic device that quickly becomes conventional. It would be so, at any rate, were it not for the diversity and subtlety of his characterization; in some cases, characterization even supplies the subject of the play, as in the *Dyskolos.*

CHARACTERS IN MENANDER'S COMEDIES

The *Dyskolos* (a fairly early comedy for Menander, dating from 316) is from beginning to end a burlesque of a cantankerous and misanthropic personality. Cnemon, a grumpy old man, has taken an aversion to his fellow men and decided to flee their company; he bullies all who approach him. This is particularly trying to Sostratus, who is in love with Cnemon's daughter. The turning point comes when Cnemon, while trying to recover a bucket and spade from the bottom of a well, falls in himself—and cannot do without the help of others for a change! As it happens, he is fished out by his stepson and Sostratus, after which he is all agreement on the subject of marriages. His personality does not change, but he at least admits his error: "I wouldn't have believed that in all the world there was a single creature capable of acting disinterestedly, out of sympathy for his neighbor."

The portrait of the "atrabilious" man is thus the very subject of the comedy. Nor can we doubt that this attempt to describe and delimit human types was characteristic of Menander. He was a friend of Theophrastus, author of the *Characters;* and we may note that some of the titles of Menander's lost plays correspond to characters in Theophrastus (*The Rustic, The Superstitious Man, The Flatterer*). Menander also bequeathed to world drama a certain number of "types," or typical characters, who were part of the society of his day and who, thanks to him, have become classic: the lover, the soldier, the sponger, the cook—and above all the slave (often named Daos), that bold and ingenious slave who lectures his young masters, comes up with expedients, and pulls the strings of the plot, all without losing a very realistic sense of where his own advantage lies. . . .

Yet the existence of these typical, recognizable characters in no way excludes variety or subtle psychological nuances; far from it. No old man, young lover, or slave is ever exactly like another. At the same time, the vicissitudes [variations] of the plot produce bursts of feeling, which are portrayed even as they arise. Politics has disappeared in the comedies of Menander; but it has been replaced by psychology. Like the tragedies of Euripides, Menander's plays are rich in monologues. Some are funny, like that of the lover in the *Dyskolos* who, having disguised himself as a farm worker, returns from the fields dog-tired, regretting his premature zeal, and yet comes back for more: "Why? I can't say, no, by the gods!" (line 544). Others are touching, like the remorseful speech of the young husband in *The Arbitrators*, who learns that his wife, whom he has accused unjustly, is faithful to him after all.

One trait characterizes Menander's world as a whole: it is a civilized and affectionate world. The misanthrope of the *Dyskolos is* something of an exception to the rule, but this is precisely because the play is intended to criticize his failing; and though his language is bitter, it is far from offensive. Likewise, Menander's slaves can be insolent and waggish, but they are no longer a pretext for the obscene jokes of which Aristophanes was so fond. Graciousness and basic courtesy almost always prevail among Menander's characters, just as a supple discretion prevails in his style. These traits faithfully reflect his ideal of human behavior.

HUMANITY IN MENANDER

The *Dyskolos* is a case in point: those who lack a sense of human solidarity owe it to themselves to acquire one. Men need one another, and the most admirable human quality is precisely that proper to man, "humanity." Cnemon lacks it, and is described as "a man with too little humanity". . . . By contrast, the man who lives up to the human ideal touches us; as a famous fragment puts it, "What a charming creature is man, when he is a man!" A number of other aphoristic lines illustrate the reciprocal ties this virtue weaves among men: "No one is a stranger to me if he is virtuous," "That's what it is to live: not to live for oneself alone". . . .

This sense of fraternity among men suits the new age, in which man's horizon is no longer bounded by the city-state; it reflects the cosmopolitanism of the philosophers who were Menander's contemporaries. But such a feeling had been expressed earlier by Aristotle; and his school may well have been the source of Menander's ideal, insofar as he recommends making a practice of mildness and tolerance. For these are the new virtues of this new world: *The Arbitrators* is an attack on impetuous anger and an example of forgiveness, understanding, and reconciliation. So is *The Shorn Girl*. The plays of Menander are constantly presenting us with family attachments, marks of affection, friendships. There is even a kind of affectionate familiarity toward slaves; and even harp girls and courtesans show signs of delicacy. The tact and grace of Menander's art are tailored to this new ideal of human relationships. The civic spirit of earlier centuries has yielded its sway to a more flexible private life, in which affection comes into its own.

These traits surely account for the considerable popularity Menander's work enjoyed . . . which was long-lived. Archaeologists have recently uncovered a whole series of mosaics in Mytilene that are illustrations of Menander's comedies; they date from around 300 and help us to picture the way the plays would have been staged at that time.

For us, Menander has eclipsed all the other writers of New Comedy—some of whom, it must be said, often bested him in the dramatic competitions during his lifetime. Philemon is the best known of these. Syracusan by birth and Athenian by adoption, he spent some time at the Egyptian court. He lived from 361 to 262. Diphilus also enjoyed great fame. Apollodorus of Carystus modeled his work closely on Menander's. All three wrote comedies that were [like Menander's] imitated by [the Roman playwrights] Plautus or Terence. Their works, of which we have only slim fragments, subscribed to the same esthetic as that reflected in Menander's—the only difference being that the first two also wrote comedies on mythological subjects, as had the poets of the preceding generation; it is characteristic of Menander that he should have avoided these.

CHAPTER 4

Greek Drama's Living Legacy

Greek
Drama

Revivals of Greek Drama in Later Ages

Margarete Bieber

After Greek drama declined in the fourth and third centuries B.C., Roman playwrights used the most popular Greek plays for inspiration in creating their own tragedies and comedies. Many centuries later, when Renaissance and modern Europeans rediscovered ancient drama, they became fascinated first by the Roman plays, and then, through them, began embracing the works of Sophocles and his contemporaries. For that reason, this overview of later revivals of Greek drama by Margarete Bieber, former scholar at Columbia and Princeton Universities, first briefly recaps the European rediscovery of Roman theater. Bieber goes on to tell how a group of Italian scholars attempting to recreate Greek plays in their original form invented a new kind of entertainment—opera (which, as it turned out, actually bears little resemblance to ancient Greek productions); and then describes a number of twentieth-century productions, both professional and college, making the point that the latter are often the most effective in capturing the spirit of the originals.

The history of the Greek and Roman theater, like the history of the whole Greek and Roman culture, is so rich and many-sided that each later period of European civilization has found some aspect of it to use as an inspiration or model for its own time. Even the periods which resented the ancient theater and the religion which underlay its productions found something to explore and to use for their own goals. Thus the mediaeval period with its distrust of everything pagan and the romantic age of the early nineteenth century with its hatred for classicizing and its nationalistic tendency, drew occasionally on ancient sources which are still living and productive today.

THE ROMANS REDISCOVERED FIRST

Although in mediaeval times the tragedy and the theater buildings of the Greeks and Romans were unknown, the Latin comedies of [the Roman playwrights] Plautus and Terence [who copied many elements of Greek comedy] remained alive. . . . The comedies of Plautus and Terence were copied and read all through mediaeval times, with Terence preferred and continuously illustrated. This, however, was done only in the monasteries and in small intellectual circles. There were no theatrical presentations and no real continuity in the study of the Latin comedy. . . .

In the Renaissance, the reawakening of ancient civilization included the study of the Latin writers Plautus [the moralist-playwright], Seneca, and [architect] Vitruvius, who were used as models for creative production. . . .

Vitruvius became the model for the theater building of the later Renaissance and the baroque period, just as Plautus and Terence had become the models for comedy and Seneca for tragedy. Vitruvius was rediscovered and printed for the first time in 1484. Up to that date there had been no special theater building. The mediaeval plays were given in the churches; the Renaissance plays in palaces, schools, and universities. . . .

The late fifteenth, the sixteenth, and the seventeenth centuries were much interested in the machinery of the ancient theater as described by Vitruvius. A linen background was fixed on a skeleton of planks and parted in the center, so that it could be drawn away to show other scenery. . . .

INCREASED INTEREST IN ANCIENT GREEK PLAYS

The study of the Latin authors during the sixteenth century was supplemented by that of the Greek authors. Aristotle's *Poetics* was read but sometimes misunderstood. He was credited with the three unities of action, place, and time. This induced the playwrights to restrict themselves to a single plot, to avoid a change of scenery, and to limit the action to not more than one day. This was in contrast to the taste of the late Renaissance and the baroque period, when audiences wanted rich shows and got them in the inter-

mezzi, given between the acts of the dramas, where scenery
could be changed at will, and discrepancies of time and
place were disregarded.

Greek Comedy was almost non-existent during the Renaissance. Menander was unknown; he had disappeared behind his Latin imitators. Aristophanes was occasionally performed in Cambridge: *Plutus* in 1536 and *Peace* in 1546. A
program drawn up for Jesuit colleges in 1551 recommends
readings from *Plutus* (the latest of Aristophanes' comedies)
in the class for beginning Greek.

The comedies of the seventeenth and eighteenth centuries
continued to use the stock characters of the Latin comedy:
the contrasting pairs of old men and of youths, the braggart
soldier, the parasite, the miser, the servant, the maid; also
the same plots: comedies of errors, mistaken identity, im-
personation, disguise. While in the seventeenth century
Plautus was favored as a model, Terence, who was nearer to
the Greek originals, became more popular in the eighteenth.

The plays by the three classical Greek tragic writers were
first printed by Aldus in Venice: Sophocles was published in
1502, Euripides in 1503, and Aeschylus in 1518. From then
on they were translated and adapted in Italy, France, and
Germany. Sophocles' *Oedipus the King* was performed in an
Italian translation at the occasion of the opening of the Teatro
Olympico in 1585. Music was used as a background. . . .

Opera, the most important creation based on the Greek
tragedies, originated at the end of the sixteenth century in
Florence. A group of scholars, poets, and musicians called
the Camerata gathered in 1594 in the palazzo of the noble-
man Giovanni Bardi. They discovered that music had played
a predominant role in ancient tragedy. Members of this
group included Vincenzo Galileo, the father of Galileo
Galilei, a musician and mathematician, much interested in
the revival of ancient music; Jacopo Peri and Guilio Caccini,
musicians; and Ottario Rinuccini, a poet. Peri and Rinuccini
collaborated in *Dafne,* performed in 1597; Caccini with both
in *Euridice,* performed in 1600. They were convinced that
they had recreated Greek tragedy. This mixture of drama,
music, and spectacle spread through all Italy, France, Aus-
tria, Germany, and England. Claudio Monteverdi performed
his *Dafne, Arianna,* and *Orfeo* at Mantua in 1607–1608.
Mythological stories in dialogue against a musical background, thought to be reincarnated Greek tragedy, became

so popular that most theaters from then on were built in large scale and with overladen decorations solely for opera. Venice had one opera house in 1637, ten more in 1700, by which time some 360 operas had been produced.

The eighteenth century is a period of great actors and singers, and opera flourished. Gluck based *Orpheus und Eurydike* (1762) on principles of the Greek drama, which he attempted to recreate. His pupil Antonio Maria Gasparo Sacchini (1772–82, active in London; 1782–86 in Paris where he died) wrote an opera, *Edipo a Colono*, based on Sophocles' last tragedy. More sumptuous theaters were built for opera: San Carlo in Naples, 1737, and La Scala in Milan, 1778. The Metropolitan Opera House in New York City still follows in general the Italian pattern. . . .

The nineteenth century is a century of classical scholarship. Much research was done, and Greek and Latin had the undisputed primary position in the curricula of high schools and universities in England as well as in Germany, Italy, and France. More and more people read the authors in the original. . . .

At the end of the nineteenth and during the first half of the twentieth century, Greek and Latin lost their leading position in education. They had to yield to more practical training in modern languages, physical science, economics, and psychology. . . . Yet the interest in Greek drama reached an unusual height in the same period.

MODERN VERSIONS OF GREEK TRAGEDY AND COMEDY

In the twentieth century the attitude of scholars and poets in reference to Greek and Latin drama has changed. In order to bring the masterpieces to a larger public than only the classicists, who became less and less interested in the languages themselves, eminent scholars translated the dramas into their native tongues. . . .

The modern poets, on the other hand, use the ancient originals as vehicles for bringing forth their own ideas of the great issues of human life: love, war, sin, tyranny, courage, fate. They preserve the outlines of the ancient myth as transmitted by the Greek tragic poets, but they alter the values, the motifs, the significance, and the results. Their own philosophy and political creeds are brought in. Thus [American playwright] Eugene O'Neill in his *Mourning Becomes Electra* uses the frame given by Aeschylus' trilogy the *Oresteia*, but the scene is laid among the Puritan aristocracy of New England in the time of the Civil War, instead of in the royal house of Mycenae at the time of the Trojan War. It has been remarked that O'Neill used the severe dramatic structure of Aeschylus' masterpiece for "a grand stupendous thriller," "his most ambitious and impressive play," and "a mechanical imitation of the Attic pattern.". . .

The French and the German writers are particularly inclined to imbue the classical dramas with political allusions. Thus Jean-Paul Sartre, in *The Flies,* written in 1943 during the Nazi occupation of France, reworks the *Eumenides* of Aeschylus in such a way that the flies represent the feeling of guilt instead of being revenging furies. Orestes does not kill his mother and her paramour out of revenge for his father, but to liberate the population of Thebes from tyranny. The moral implication is that France must achieve self-reliance and assume a sense of responsibility. [French playwright Jean] Anouilh has reworked Sophocles' *Antigone* (1942) in a similar sense. This play was produced in Paris at the time when it was occupied by the Germans. The framework of Sophocles was retained, but the leading characters were changed. The criticism of the tyrant is so subtle that the Nazis did not grasp the significance. When this play was presented by Cedric Hardwicke on Broadway in 1946 . . . the idea of protest was not brought out. Therefore neither public nor critics understood that politics had replaced religion. The audiences were bored and the play closed rather quickly, despite the great art of Katharine Cornell as Antigone. The impression of dullness was increased by the commentator who substituted in this play for the chorus, by the introduction of the nurse who is a Euripidean character, and by everyday dress, particularly the kind of housecoat for Antigone and an evening coat for Creon instead of the beautiful Greek dresses. More authentic dresses were used in another representation of the same play in the off-Broadway production of the Circle-in-the-Square Theater at Sheridan Square in Greenwich Village in 1951. Even if Creon had not worn the swastika, the veiled allusion to the problems of the Hitler era came out very well. . . .

The *Medea* of Euripides was adapted by Anouilh in 1946, translated into English by Robinson Jeffers, and staged by John Gielgud in 1947–1949 on Broadway. The translation, the production, and the great art of Judith Anderson all showed a tendency toward the Senecan spirit. Instead of the tragic grandeur of a deceived and humbled proud woman, only the jealousy of a disappointed loving wife was worked out. . . . Great modern actresses like Judith Anderson are inclined to the more pathetic style of Seneca; recently a retired Broadway actress, playing the *Medea* of Euripides on the Columbia campus, insisted upon inserting one speech from Seneca into the Euripidean text. The idea of Medea, the fate of a foreigner in a hostile land, was also used by Maxwell Anderson in his *Wingless Victory* (1937). . . .

While the humor and stage efficiency of Plautus is indestructible, the representative of Greek Old Comedy, Aristophanes, does not lend himself to modern adaptations and cannot be understood without a thorough study of the political, cultural, and literary circumstances under which he wrote. The *Lysistrata*, made into a farce from the Greek of Aristophanes . . . and produced by the Philadelphia Theatre Association in New York City, 1930–31, reached 252 performances. When, however, the *Lysistrata* was made into a "movie" in Vienna and announced in New York in 1948 as "The Battle of the Sexes," it became . . . a deserved failure. The same is true of the recent attempts to rewrite and produce the *Thesmophoriazusae* and the *Ecclesiazusae* of Aristophanes. . . .

Menander, the newly-discovered representative of Greek New Comedy, in contrast to Aristophanes, lends himself beautifully to modern presentations. . . . An excellent and enjoyable performance of the newly found *Dyskolos* by Menander was given by the students of Fordham University in New York, in the translation by Gilbert Highet, in 1960. I believe that the plays by Menander have a meaning for modern audiences and a great future in the theater . . . for their human qualities appeal to human nature at all times. . . .

PROFESSIONAL AND COLLEGE PRODUCTIONS IN MANY COUNTRIES

Performances of Greek [drama] could be seen in . . . Greece, Italy, France, Germany, Holland, England, and in the United States, mostly in good translations into the respective languages, but sometimes even in the original or modern Greek. This was the case in the impressive performances produced . . . in the ancient theater in Delphi in 1927 and 1930. The back part of the orchestra was raised and temporarily built into a kind of podium. Here Prometheus in Aeschylus' *Pro-*

metheus was seen bound to a rock, which was supposed to blend with the mountains in the background. The chorus . . . in the orchestra was sometimes turned toward him, with their backs to the spectators, lifting their hands while singing to him. In the same place the *Suppliants,* the oldest tragedy of Aeschylus known to us, was performed in 1930. The chorus, which here has the leading part, performed various movements and dances in the orchestra . . . The actors wore masks and long flowing robes. . . .

The *Persians* was performed with masks in Frankfurt and without masks . . . in the ancient Theater of Herodes Atticus in Athens in 1930. *The Seven against Thebes* was given in Ostia in 1927, where also the *Antigone* by Sophocles and the *Clouds* by Aristophanes were presented.

The favorite drama by Aeschylus for modern presentation is, however, the *Agamemnon.* It was given in Greek in Delphi in 1930 and in Italian in the ancient theater of Syracuse in 1914. . . .

The whole *Oresteia—Agamemnon, Choephorae,* and *Eumenides—*was given in 1954 in Greek in the Randolph-Macon College at Lynchburg, Virginia. This college has performed Greek plays each year since 1909, all in the Greek language. Besides the *Oresteia,* the *Electra* of Sophocles, the *Medea* and *The Trojan Women* of Euripides, and the *Birds* of Aristophanes were performed against improvised backgrounds with great success. Fordham University in New York City also performed Greek drama in the original language prior to World War II. The whole *Oresteia* was reduced to one hour for a presentation on television in January 1959 in New York. Even in this compressed version some scenes, for example the return of Agamemnon, made a great impression. . . .

Oedipus the King is a favorite with modern actors and stage managers. Laurence Olivier of the Old Vic in London, England, gave a truly tragic performance on Broadway in 1946 in this play. The proud behavior in the beginning, the turning from confidence to fear, the despair at the end, made this a memorable recreation of the Greek spirit. . . .

The students of the Catholic University of America in Washington presented an adaptation of *Oedipus the King* . . . in many colleges in America, and in April 1959 it was performed in Carnegie Hall, New York. The chorus spoke clearly and melodiously. The deep meaning of Sophocles' masterpiece was well transmitted. . . .

Greek tragedies have been presented in [modern times] in ancient Greek theaters—Epidaurus (festivals since 1954), Delphi, Syracuse . . . modern theaters—in New York City on Broadway and off Broadway and in the Brander Matthews Theater at Columbia University, in Berlin in the Grosse Schauspielhaus and the Deutsche Theater, in Frankfurt, Cassel, Mainz, Giessen, in modern open-air theaters—in Reading, England, in Holland, in American colleges like Cedar Crest, Elizabeth, California . . . in the circus, in community halls and barns. The best productions were those where chorus and actors acted together in the orchestra before a palace out of which, as in ancient times, the main actors stepped. When, however, the managers tried to present a scene simultaneously on the stage and in the orchestra, the attempt was not successful, or was even ridiculous, and sometimes confusing. The old mistaken idea, that the actors performed on the stage while at the same time the chorus sang and danced in the orchestra, has definitely to be discarded. The idea that one or a few speakers can be substituted for the chorus is a false one; the result is always unsatisfactory.

Aside from those already named, other American colleges and universities are also active in stage production and have done much to improve the revivals of Greek plays. A partial list might include the following: Vassar College, Reed College in Portland, Oregon; Northwestern University; the Pacific Little Theater in Stockton and several other California theaters.

Barnard College, the college for girls at Columbia University, has a specialty in the reviving of the Greek spirit. Each year they have Greek Games, in which they attempt to reproduce, as nearly as modern conditions permit, a classical festival. It is built around some story of Greek mythology, dealing with some god or hero like Athena, Apollo, Orpheus, Hephaestus. The chorus sings the story which, however, is also acted in short mimetic scenes. Story, songs, music, dances and costumes are created by the girls themselves. A contest in dance is followed by the athlete's oath to Zeus and to the god or hero to whom the games are dedicated. There follow contests in discus throwing, jumping of hurdles, hoop rolling, a chariot race, and a torch race. . . .

THE SPIRIT OF GREEK DRAMA

The scene of action for modern presentations thus has been everything from the Greek orchestra to the . . . modern stage, or a primitive stage erected in the open air or in a hall. In most cases the modern stage is used. This is quite satisfactory, as the Romans not only produced Greek plays on their stage, but had the forms of the Greek theater building adapted to their needs. The form of the Roman theater is indeed the underlying foundation of our theater building today. . . .

The Greek theater was an open-air theater. When it is possible, as in Athens, Epidaurus, Syracuse, and Delphi, to use the ancient theater, the presentation in the round orchestra with a background building will be of great value. But the theater building had only its first development in Greece, was perfected by the Romans, and still challenges our modern theater buildings. Any theater, therefore, can be used for the presentation of Greek drama. It does not make much difference whether the drama is presented in the open air, on a meadow, in a barn, in a circus, in a museum or university auditorium, in an ancient theater or in a sophisticated, modern theater building. The modern attempts at central staging, as in the theater of the Circle-in-the-Square in New York, or in a projected theater for the University of Arkansas, are really a return to the original and primitive idea of the dramatic dance in religious performances. The audiences stood or sat on all sides of the Greek threshing floor and the Roman circus, which were the places of action before Aeschylus and Sophocles in Athens and Plautus in Rome needed background scenery on one side and the audience concentrated on the opposite side. Wherever a clever director and responsive actors absorb the spirit of Greek drama, the eternal value of its heroic greatness and vitality will be brought to the surface and stir the emotions of a cultivated audience regardless of the outer surroundings.

Enduring Fascination for *Oedipus the King*

Charles R. Walker

Sophocles' *Oedipus the King,* the riveting story of a man who unknowingly kills his father, marries his mother, and meets his downfall when he discovers the truth, has often been called not only the greatest Greek dramatic work, but also the greatest tragedy ever written. And the title character, who also appears in Sophocles' sequel, *Oedipus at Colonus,* has, through the ages, fascinated both play producers and playgoers, as well as novelists, psychologists, and other thinkers. In this essay, excerpted from the introduction to his translations of the two Oedipus plays, noted theatrical scholar and translator Charles R. Walker presents a detailed overview of how succeeding generations have been drawn to the character of Oedipus and to the tortured events of his timeless story.

If it were possible to count all the performances of *Oedipus the King* since its first showing at the theater of Dionysus on the side of the Acropolis in 429 B.C., it would undoubtedly emerge as the most continuously produced play in dramatic history. As to its reputation as a masterpiece—not to mention the ink spent to explain it—it competes with [Shakespeare's] *Hamlet.* But something quite new has happened to *Oedipus,* as theater, since the Second World War. This ancient story of incest and murder is now known, because of Freud and the "Oedipus complex," to millions of men and women in the modern world. Familiarity with the outline of the story, however, is, at most, only a contributory cause to the triumphal re-entry of Sophocles' play into the theaters of Europe, England, and the United States. . . . I have been convinced that *Oedipus* and other Greek plays have begun to

Excerpted from Charles R. Walker, *Sophocles' "Oedipus the King" and "Oedipus at Colonus"* (Garden City, NY: Doubleday). Copyright ©1966 by Charles R. Walker. Reprinted with permission from the author.

speak to the modern world with the authority of living theater. How and why has this happened?

Oedipus the King, aside from its subtleties of poetry and theme, is, of course, superb theater. It has the kind of hard, bony structure that can withstand almost any degree of bad direction and acting. But there are elements other than sheer theatrical effectiveness which account for its power. These relate to the mythical material out of which Sophocles and other ancient dramatists constructed their plays, material which has continued to attract writers up to the present day.

Here, however, we shall be concerned chiefly with *Oedipus* as theater, past and present. . . .

MARCHING THROUGH THE CENTURIES

Sophocles wrote *Oedipus the King* at the height of his career as a dramatist. Although Aristotle, a century later, chose it as the masterpiece of Greek tragedy, this most durable of Greek plays did not, at its initial showing, receive first prize. We know that Sophocles wrote what might be called the last act of the Oedipus drama, *Oedipus at Colonus,* years later. I shall argue that *Oedipus the King* needs this last act and that, in terms of both theater and the underlying myth, the two plays should be performed together to be fully understood.

After the great period of Greek drama the Oedipus story continued to march vigorously through the centuries. Talented actors in all ages have been especially attracted to the role of Oedipus. Polus, for example, the most famous actor of the fourth century, was especially renowned for his performances in both *Oedipus the King* and *Oedipus at Colonus.* During the fourth century B.C. the level of dramatic writing had declined, while the art of acting and the importance of individual actors rose. In fact, as actors became more influential they tended to modify classical dramas in order to give themselves more attractive roles. Finally Lycurgus, who was famous for rebuilding the theater of Dionysus and for his patronage of the ancient drama, put a stop to this tampering with Athens' classical heritage by ordering that state copies of all the tragedies be deposited in the archives and that a fine be imposed on anyone who changed the scripts. . . .

Greece fell under Roman rule in 146 B.C., but the Greek theater maintained a quasi-independence and enjoyed immense popularity throughout the empire well into the second century A.D. From what records we have of Roman productions, the story of Oedipus—in Sophocles' version as well as others—continued an active life in the theater of the Graeco-Roman world for another four hundred years. Classical scholars are fond of noting that Julius Caesar as a young man tried his hand as a playwright and wrote his own *Oedipus Rex*. The Emperor Nero acted Oedipus in a production of the Sophoclean play, and Seneca wrote a very dull but influential *Oedipus Rex*. Though Seneca introduced as much gore as might be expected from a gladiatorial combat, he managed to produce at the same time the least dramatic of all the extant [surviving] versions.

In the so-called Dark Ages, Greek tragedies faded from the consciousness of the West, although they continued to be performed for several centuries in the Byzantine Empire. A fragment of a bas-relief in the Hermitage, circa A.D. 500, shows scenes from *Medea* and *Oedipus*, and there are records of other performances to the end of the seventh century.

Early in the fifteenth century, Greek tragedies in manuscript began to reach Italy—brought by adventurous scholars from Byzantium. The most famous of these scholars, Giovanni Aurispa, literally sold the clothes off his back in Constantinople in order to bring back to Venice a booty of two hundred and thirty-eight manuscripts, including six tragedies of Aeschylus and seven of Sophocles. These tragedians as well as Euripides were edited and printed by Aldus, the Venetian scholar and Hellenist [enthusiast of Greek culture]. Sophocles was the first to be published, in 1502.

LAUNCHED IN THE MODERN THEATER

The modern theatrical life of *Oedipus the King* may be said to have begun rather precisely in Vicenza on March 3, 1585, when the Sophoclean tragedy was performed amid much pomp at the opening of the famous Teatro Olimpico of Palladio. The play was presented in an admirable Italian translation by the Venetian scholar and statesman Orsatto Giustiniani, with music by Andrea Gabrieli, organist at the Cathedral of San Marco. "It was fitting," wrote Filippo Pigafetta, a member of the first audience, "that this most renowned theater in the world should have as its first presentation the most excellent tragedy in the world.". . .

With the 1585 Vicenza performance, *Oedipus* was launched in the modern theater. Later, in the classical period of the

French theater, Corneille wrote his own version, adding a love plot. Racine considered competing with Sophocles, but refrained. Voltaire wrote an *Oedipe*, turning the play into an anticlerical tract, with the prophet Tiresias a venal and corrupt priest. . . .

In England, Dryden and Lee wrote a translation of Sophocles' *Oedipus*, effectively bowdlerizing [removing and censoring] all the shocking elements of the plot. Only in the nineteenth century, however, did *Oedipus* really begin his return to the modern theater—in preparation, it might be said, for something far more explosive and significant in the twentieth century. Performances in ancient Greek began to multiply in the universities in the middle of the nineteenth century and have continued up to the present day. There were many notable performances in the United States, in England, and on the Continent. Sir Richard Jebb, greatest of English Sophoclean scholars, crossed the Atlantic in 1888 to see the play given at Harvard. He includes an account of it in his famous—and still the best—edition of the play. Whether in the original or in the vernacular [translations], these performances in the theater introduced a new idea of Greek plays, an idea which seemed revolutionary and positively subversive to some classical scholars: that *Oedipus* and other Greek plays could only be fully understood in the theater, not in the library! The idea is still scorned by a dwindling number of regressive classicists. As part of this modernization movement, translations appeared in more or less speakable versions, often to the horror of the purely philological [those obsessed with the original wording].

Perhaps the two most famous productions of *Oedipus* in the late nineteenth and early twentieth centuries were those of the great French actor Mounet-Sully and of the German producer Max Reinhardt. Members of the audience who saw his performance say that Mounet-Sully's Oedipus was the greatest theatrical experience of their lives. In a generation when great actors played all the leading roles in the classics, from Shakespeare to Ibsen, Mounet-Sully believed his Oedipus to be (and he is supported by the testimony of contemporary critics) his greatest role. Mounet-Sully's first performance of *Oedipus* took place in a Roman amphitheater in the south of France; he was to play that role for many years, well into the twentieth century. He even made a silent movie of the play, without cutting the original.

Reinhardt's *Oedipus* exploded on the scene in 1910 in the Circus Schumann in Berlin, and again in 1919 in the gigantic Grosse Schulspielhaus. Though it used a German translation of Sophocles' text, the production was sheer Reinhardt, a mighty spectacle, complete with milling crowds and fervent realism in scenic and sound effects. Later, Reinhardt brought his production to England.

One theatergoer who was present at both the Mounet-Sully and the Reinhardt productions was J.T. Sheppard, the distinguished Greek scholar, then a young man and fellow of King's College, Cambridge. His comments were obviously written out of emotion, and with ideas that came to him in the theater and not in his Cambridge study.

Of Reinhardt's production he wrote: "That performance taught me that the strength of the plot makes the play great and exciting even in the worst conditions that a bad producer can invent."

Of Mounet-Sully's performance, which he saw in Paris, he said: "Because of its formal beauty, the French production is an inspiration to all who care for drama, and a proof that Greek drama, not bolstered up by sensationalism and with sentimentality, has power to hold and to move a modern audience. If you doubt whether in these days Greek tragedy still matters, you may learn the answer in Paris.". . .

A TOWERING PRODUCTION

The real *Oedipus* explosion, however, both in translation and performance, came only after the Second World War. Popular reading of Greek tragedy in translation has increased prodigiously in all Western countries. . . . In number of translations and in number of readers the English language leads all the rest, although excellent new versions are appearing in French, Italian, and modern Greek. . . .

[An] example of a towering modern production is that of Minotis and the Greek National Theater. Alexis Minotis has directed and acted in *Oedipus the King* in Greece, in the United States, in France, in Italy, and at the Edinburgh Theater festival. But it is only at the ancient Greek theater at Epidaurus that one can fully experience Minotis' *Oedipus.*

To begin with, the setting is dramatic and beautiful: fifty-five tiers of seats rise against Mt. Kynortion and look out over an expanse of tall cypresses and olive groves, where lie the ruins of a temple to Aesculapius and a vast complex of other

buildings devoted to his cult and the cure of the sick. Epidaurus is famous for having the best-preserved round orchestra
of any of the theaters of antiquity. In the center is the stone
"thymele," or altar, which even today no Greek actor dare
desecrate by stepping on. A two-story stage has been recon-
structed on the far side, where most of the dialogue is spoken.
The audience gathers slowly; there are tourists from abroad,
but they lose themselves in the crowd. Front-row seats are reserved, as in Sophocles' time, for Greek and foreign digni-
taries, but Greeks of all classes arrive in big American-built
cars and in ramshackle local buses. Peasant women in black
skirts with white kerchiefs round their heads come with their
mustached men. They climb the fifty-five tiers to the cheaper
seats, but the miraculous acoustics of the theater bring every
word of the play even to those in the last rows. . . .

Here are a few of my impressions of Minotis' production,
based on what I wrote down immediately after:

"Unimaginable force and fury in Oedipus' drive for the secret which he knows will mean his destruction. You see it
causing him to threaten the old herdsman, first with words
and then with physical pain. The shepherd's crook falls clat-
tering to the ground and he begins to speak. . . .

"As the herdsman approaches the final telling, Oedipus
goes behind the old man and tensely seizes his shoulders.
Suddenly all difference in age, education, and rank between
king and slave fall away; they become one in the terrible
bond of their secret. In the last speech, revealing Oedipus'
fate, the old man slowly reaches back and puts one hand on
the hand of Oedipus, the man whom he has saved from
death—yet for the most terrible of human destinies. Then a
great cry from Oedipus—like a sword thrust—and the un-
forgettable speech, 'All true, all clear . . .'

"The final scene of the play, when Oedipus enters
blinded—a scene that so many translators . . . have declared
is too horrible to be borne by a modern audience—is the
most absorbing and somehow the most satisfying in the
whole tragedy. Here the audience seems wholly to lose itself
in the counterpoint of Oedipus' emotions and in the purga-
tion of pity and terror which they share with him."

APPEALING TO MODERN HOPES AND FEARS

So much for a compressed record of twenty-five centuries of
Oedipus the King. What accounts for this remarkable dura-

bility? And what explains the return of *Oedipus* with renewed vigor into the theatrical world of the twentieth century?

Dramatic critics, from Aristotle on, have celebrated the uncanny ingenuity displayed by Sophocles in articulating his plots. And this surely is one reason for the *Oedipus* vitality. Shakespeare's plays have often been praised for their range of theatrical appeal, from pit to gallery. Whatever its other dimensions, the *Oedipus* of Sophocles may be enjoyed by the pit as a great whodunit whose plot exhibits great ingenuity in combining a maximum of horror and suspense as the protagonist tracks down the murderer. As to the play's architecture, scholars and critics have always admired its dramatic virtuosity and power. And in recent years the sharper psychological tools of modern criticism have added new levels of meaning as critics have sought to explore the depths of the ancient myth and Sophocles' treatment of it. . . .

More important than the superb plot—or, rather, inseparable from it—is the dynamism of the Sophoclean theme imbedded in it. As in *Hamlet*, men have always found half a dozen "universal" themes emerging from the play. To some of those in *Oedipus*, I would argue, the modern world is particularly responsive—a statement, incidentally, which applies to more than one Greek tragedy. In this play we are in the presence of a complex appeal—and challenge—to both the hopes and fears of modern man.

Who am I? Man searches for himself. What makes that eternal theme so penetrating and, in certain ways, so new to us in Sophocles' play? The key lies, I think, in certain curiously modern characteristics in Oedipus' personality and in his relation to his world. The reader may ask: What about those oracles, prophecies, gods, curses, pollutions, and all the other antique apparatus of the story? They certainly are not modern. No, but they melt somehow into credibility when seen through a supremely modern personality. Oedipus is a man of action, a successful leader with superior intelligence, possessed of extraordinary courage both physical and moral. However, if this were all, he would not interest us. Oedipus is an activist, but not an extrovert. His struggle for self-knowledge—and for mastery over his fears—is his passion and his destiny. One of his traits isn't common among us—to seek the truth at all costs—but the greatest scientists have taught us to admire such fortitude. From his first to his last appearance on the stage, Oedipus is pre-

sented by Sophocles as a man buffeted between the deduc-
tions of his admirable intellect and a whole psychological
showcase of unconscious fears. Most of the latter are so
deeply imbedded that only the most traumatic events can
summon them to the surface of consciousness and make
them live for us dramatically. But Sophocles summons them
all. . . . There are two parallel plots in *Oedipus the King*, as all
great actors playing the role of Oedipus have perceived: the
plot of the hidden emotions rising from a graded series of
unconscious depths and the defendant-prosecutor plot of external events. The interpenetration [fusing together] of the
two, masterfully achieved, is what makes the play great—
and new.

Ancient Greek Drama Is Still Relevant

Karelisa V. Hartigan

This essay, by Karelisa V. Hartigan, a professor of classics at the University of Florida, effectively explores the reasons that the plays of Sophocles and his fellow Greek dramatists still move audiences. Some of the same political, intellectual, and social issues that affected the ancient Greeks, Hartigan points out, continue to affect modern nations and peoples. Among these are the right of political protest, the search for the truth, the futility of war, compassion for war's victims, the consuming power of revenge, male social dominance and the resultant suffering of women, and many others.

Greek tragedy has had a continuous appeal for the American commercial theater for the last hundred years. Although the tendency of our country is to hail the new and reject the old, the Greek dramas are still brought to the stage. The theme or message of the plays by Aeschylus, Sophocles, and Euripides has consistently been deemed important, because the issues addressed by the writers of fifth-century B.C. Athens continue to be current, continue to have a relevance for twentieth-century America. Only the form, not the content, of the texts has limited the number of productions: directors find the lengthy speeches and the lack of physical action too restricting, while the ever-present chorus is difficult to use effectively.

Whenever a director or producer determines to offer a Greek tragedy, or an actress wishes to portray one of the great figures of Athenian drama, the theater critics flock to the performance. Whether or not they finally acclaim the production, almost without fail they devote much of their review to the importance of the event, and reiterate to their

Excerpted from *Greek Tragedy on the American Stage*, by Karelisa V. Hartigan. Copyright ©1995 by Karelisa V. Hartigan. Reproduced with permission from Greenwood Publishing Group, Inc., Westport, Conn.

readers a single theme: Greek drama is worth seeing. The passion displayed by these mythic characters lies at the heart of all our emotions, proclaim the critics; the choices the characters face and the decisions they make offer valuable examples to the modern audience. At times a Greek tragedy has been hailed as the best play of a contemporary theater season. But even when a show is panned, the negative reviews arise not from the play but from the production.

THE QUEST FOR THE TRUTH

Over the years the interpretation of these ancient texts has varied. Directors and producers have seen different messages in the plays, and critical reception of the performances has also changed. . . .

When Sophocles' *Oedipus Tyrannus* was first performed in 1882 [for example], it was attacked as having an immoral theme, that the actions condoned (if not actually seen onstage) would have been banned from the stage were the script not one of the "classics." In the early decades of the twentieth century, this play became one respected not only for the classroom but also for the theater. The American audience came to realize the events described in Sophocles' play have little to do with the drama's meaning, that the power of this first and, to some minds, greatest, detective story lies in Oedipus' relentless quest for the truth, a truth that brings him to realize his own identity. Post-Freudian society understood the value of facing the darkest fears of the psyche, even if these are also the strongest taboos of civilization; healing could come through recognition. When Laurence Olivier gave his famous wail of understanding (1946), he initiated this interpretation of Sophocles' play. As the years unrolled, Oedipus' quest took on even further meaning; the play came to mean not only a quest for self-identity, but it also offered an example of social responsibility: the Theban king's knowledge could heal both his own ignorance and the ills of his city. Oedipus became the scapegoat and thus the savior of his society.

The latter interpretation arose from the anthropological interests that came to popularity in the 1960s and 1970s. In tune with this new attention to the early rituals of society, the directors of Greek drama attempted to emphasize in their staging the more primitive elements that could be discovered in the texts. If these were not obvious, they were

added; thus the Burgess-Langham *Oedipus* at the Guthrie [Theater] in 1972 began with a new prologue showing human sacrifice. After this desperate attempt, the cure would then lie in the hands of the king. Oedipus as savior involved social responsibility as well as self-recognition. After nearly a century of production, *Oedipus Tyrannus* had attained success in the American commercial theater. Far from representing a moral failure, as it did in 1882, in the later years of the 1900s the Theban king's search was an exemplar of moral victory.

THEMES SEEMINGLY TORN FROM THE HEADLINES

Although Sophocles' play is arguably the most familiar drama from ancient Greece, it has not appeared recently on the commercial stage, and we might ponder why this is so. A simple answer might be that it is too well known; it is not a play that can be done in modern dress, and its primitive elements have been played too often. More contemporary directors have been turning to less well-known plays: *Ajax*, *Hecuba,* and *Persians* are the plays of recent years. It has long been recognized that the legend of Oedipus is one that cannot be retold; a modern playwright has difficulty putting a new spin on this story, so there are few, if any, modern versions of this myth. But I think the lack of interest in this play rests on a deeper foundation. *Oedipus Tyrannus* is now interpreted as a play of social and personal responsibility, and these are not popular traits in contemporary American culture. Self-knowledge as a virtue no longer holds pride of place in the current national psyche. On the other hand, if Sophocles' play is reconsidered as a drama that displays the ultimate victim, an innocent plaything doomed by the misdeeds of his parents and the inscrutable plans of the gods, I predict it will return to the stage. While I cannot argue that Sophocles intended *his* audience to understand his play thusly, neither could he have foreseen that the audiences of 1882 would condemn its morality.

The same lack of interest in social ills underlies, I think, the lesser appeal of *Antigone,* although the 1994 staging of this play by A.C.T. [American Conservatory Theater] in San Francisco reveals the text still has meaning. . . . In 1946 the world was recovering from the madness of a political tyrant [Adolf Hitler], and *Antigone,* in [French playwright Jean] Anouilh's version, addressed how an individual might stand

against such rulers. But, as we have seen, the play's message fell on deaf ears in this country; postwar America did not care for this theme . . . [and] critical reception was cool. By 1971, however, the United States had seen and approved of political protest, and *Antigone* at the Vivian Beaumont [Theater] was hailed as both timeless and immediate, a play whose plot and theme seemed torn from the daily headlines.

Twenty-three years later, A.C.T.'s [Carey] Perloff held a different view. She saw in Antigone's character a defiant young woman, yes, but also one who had to believe in her image of her family to survive the horrors of her childhood. Whereas in earlier years Antigone was believed to offer a model for public action by her stand against the state, this was not the primary concept underlying the most recent production of *Antigone*. In 1994, Antigone had become a victim of her past and her society, and her defiance was as much to prove her self-worth as to prove Creon's tyranny wrong. . . .

WAR AND REVENGE

Protest against military action, however, has remained a popular theme throughout the century. From the first staging of Euripides' *Trojan Women* in 1915 to Peter Sellar's production of Sophocles' *Ajax* in 1986, the plays that point out the suffering of war continue to appeal. There is no mystery here: the horrors of human conflict and the pain of its victims continue unabated, while the words of those who speak out against it are usually spoken in vain. In the production history of *Trojan Women*, the only time the tragedy lacked appeal was during the "happy days" of the 1950s. At all other moments when the play appeared on the American stage, the critics unanimously proclaimed that Euripides understood and expressed the vanities of war.

Ajax, while it is a play that shows how an individual can suffer at the hands of the "military establishment," and thus illustrates the victimization of the hero, also portrays how the maddened man feels guilt for his deeds and ends his life to avoid further humiliation. As I suggested above in regard to *Oedipus*, this is not a popular theme in modern America. As there have been no productions of Euripides' *Heracles*, another play in which the hero takes responsibility for his actions done in madness (even if sent by a god), so *Ajax* has been staged only once. As a play that speaks against the military establishment, it has appeal; as a text that celebrates

personal responsibility, it does not. The tragic grandeur of Oedipus, Heracles, or Ajax, victims of uncaring gods but facing their destinies with courage, cannot shine through that basic issue of personal responsibility.

Revenge is a theme that continues to hold appeal on the contemporary American stage. *Medea* and stories from the House of Atreus have been "granted a chorus" throughout the period of this study. In the early years of the century, Euripides' *Medea* and Sophocles' *Electra* were chosen as vehicles by an actress wishing to play a role that tested her dramatic ability. . . .

For *Medea* the lure of the role itself has remained the motivating factor; the theme of Euripides' text has not seemed to trouble either those onstage or those in the audience overly much. While the drama critics at the earliest performances . . . were somewhat put off by the heroine's violent retaliation, they chalked up her fury to her barbarian nature: Medea may be the heroine of a Greek play, but she is a foreigner. In more recent times, directors have made an attempt to focus upon Medea as victim of chauvinist men; Jason is easily recognized even by those who do not consider themselves feminists. Medea's act of revenge thus springs from this victimization. Once again, when the ancient text can be interpreted on the personal, rather than the social level, then it plays well on the modern stage. Sophocles' *Philoctetes,* for example, has seldom been offered, because although the hero is clearly a victim and exiled through no fault of his own, his healing and his glory depend upon his return to society, the very society that wronged him. Philoctetes is allowed no personal revenge against those responsible for his suffering, while Medea takes the ultimate revenge and is exalted for taking it. . . .

Let us return now to *Electra* and the other plays arising from the House of Atreus legend, all but one based on the theme of revenge. The performance history of Sophocles' *Electra* begins early, and the play continues to be performed regularly. The other texts based on this myth, *Oresteia, Orestes,* and *Iphigeneia at Aulis,* however, did not appear on the American stage until midway in the twentieth century. The first full productions of Aeschylus' *Oresteia,* for instance, were at Ypsilanti, Michigan, in summer 1966, and at the Guthrie Theater in the fall of that year. A separate staging of Euripides' *Orestes* first took place two years later, while his

Iphigeneia at Aulis . . . was not "granted a chorus" until 1967. In recent years, however, it is these plays that have held pride of place among Greek dramas in the commercial theaters of the United States. . . .

With the dawn of the 1980s plays from the House of Atreus myth moved into the spotlight. First to appear was the Barton-Cavander epic ten-play presentation *The Greeks*. . . . Here the intent was to present the entire myth as a sequential package, so that audiences could see the growing power of the curse and the revenge, how the wrongs of one generation spread into and infected the next. By placing *Iphigeneia at Aulis* as the prologue, Agamemnon's guilt was brought to the fore; he did not die for Clytemnestra's whim; her revenge was aptly motivated by the king's wanton actions done in his desire for glory. This massive production was imported— and shortened—from the London stage, and toured the United States; by the time it reached the West Coast, the plays had become so altered that one critic suggested the show be retitled *The Greeks Go to Hollywood.*

It can be no accident that the opening years of the 1990s have seen three productions of the full *Oresteia*, plus a very popular interpretation of *Orestes* alone. In 1992 Ariane Mnouchkine brought to America her Théâtre du Soleil's epic staging of the trilogy, plus *Iphigeneia at Aulis*, and the performance won instant (if at times exhausted!) acclaim. In the same year the Guthrie staged its three-part version of the story, this time focusing on Clytemnestra, while in 1994 Tim Robbins' Actors' Gang Theater also offered a House of Atreus trilogy; neither included *Eumenides*. Mnouchkine's *Les Atrides* makes the myth both timeless and multicultural, but the emphasis is on the importance of women in civilization, on the part they play in this great legend and thus in the collective consciousness of contemporary society. The Guthrie's trilogy (*Iphigeneia at Aulis, Agamemnon,* and Sophocles' *Electra*) also focused on the women, but on Clytemnestra's proper action in taking revenge against the man who had wronged her (and her daughter); this was to be a feminist portrayal of Aeschylus' text. The suffering of women and their condoned personal revenge is the interpretation currently given to the play that in Aeschylus' day celebrated the institution of civic justice and the closing of vendetta law.

Tim Robbins' trilogy (*Agamemnon,* Sophocles' *Electra,* and

Orestes) was set in the modern world, with no attempt to evoke the ancient palaces. The scripts were also new: Charles Mee was author of the first and last, Ellen McLaughlin adapted Sophocles' text. Critics hailed the relevance of the play(s), since domestic violence run amok rang true for the American audiences of the 1990s. The insane asylum that was the setting for *Orestes* was also proclaimed as an appropriate metaphor for the times: in the ruins of the House of Atreus lies the deterioration, if not the collapse, of modern society.

TIMELESS SOCIAL ISSUES

Greek plays of revenge and ruin are thought to reflect the temper of the times in the contemporary commercial theater. It is certainly no accident that performances of *Medea* and stories from the House of Atreus are currently popular on the American stage. In earlier years of our century, these dramas were considered illustrative of the higher aspects of the soul. Today these plays are understood to illuminate the negative qualities of the human psyche. Such wide discrepancies are not new: the ancient playwrights also found different meanings in the myths. At the midpoint of fifth-century B.C. Athens, Aeschylus was celebrating the liberation of his democratic society from the dangers of vendetta justice, the creation of a jury court system that would deny the validity of personal revenge, and used the House of Atreus legend as the foundation for his ideas. Fifty years later, Euripides put a different spin on this myth. He still denied the validity of personal revenge, but showed in his *Orestes* that the stain of murder can drive a man and those associated with him into madness. He thought that Athens of 408 B.C. was a society sick with its political and military problems; he could only hope that his despair might be translated into positive action. Charles Mee's updated version of Euripides' play is thus on target when it is set within an insane asylum, and although its images are drawn from popular culture, we can hope, perhaps, that his play will be viewed as a warning, not a celebration, and that its message will have more power than did the Greek playwright's in his own day.

In ancient Athens, the playwright's texts reflected the current political scene and dealt with contemporary social issues. . . . performances of Greek tragedy in contemporary America also respond to social conditions, while the interpretations of the myth vary with the concerns of society. As

Aeschylus used the House of Atreus myth to celebrate the deeds of his city-state in 458 B.C., Euripides turned to the same tale in 408 B.C. to condemn its actions. In twentieth-century America, Oedipus' story illustrated a man's quest for self-knowledge when staged in the first half of the era, his responsibility to his society as its scapegoat in later years. Euripides' *Bacchae* reflected current emphasis on free love when staged in the 1960s, responded to a quest for balance in the 1980s. Only *Trojan Women* has remained constant in its message. From the day when Euripides penned it in 415 B.C. to the present time, the suffering he portrayed of war's innocent victims has spoken to audiences in nearly every decade of the past century, for the pain of military conflict is apparently neverending.

Ideas of morality, the right of political protest, the quest for self-identity, the validity of revenge, the nature of sacrifice and the need for it: the Greek tragedies address all these issues. Concepts about these issues, however, constantly change with a society's altering circumstances. But in the unchanging texts of the ancient Greek playwrights, twentieth-century directors and producers find a meaning that has validity, a message they can interpret for their audience, for their own society. From our knowledge of the Greek plays, whether we finally approve of a particular presentation or think it misses the mark, we can recognize its intent. The dramas of the Athenian playwrights address timeless issues of society and the human psyche. During the past century these unchanging texts have been brought continuously to the American stage, and, I fearlessly predict, Greek tragedies will continue to be "granted a chorus" for the contemporary theaters of our nation.

CHRONOLOGY

ca. 850–750

The epic poems the *Iliad* and the *Odyssey*, whose stories and characters will later become popular elements of Greek drama, are, according to tradition, composed by the legendary bard Homer.

ca. 566

The ancient Athenians introduce recitation contests, one of the forerunners of formal drama, in at least one of their religious festivals.

ca. 550–530

The world's first formal theater is built in Athens; its exact location remains unknown.

534

Athens first holds the City Dionysia, a religious festival honoring the fertility god Dionysus; Thespis, whom tradition credits as the first actor, wins the festival's dramatic contest.

ca. 508

A popular leader named Cleisthenes engineers the world's first democracy in Athens.

501

Comedies first appear on the program at the City Dionysia, although they are not yet officially recognized and no prizes for this new genre are yet awarded.

ca. 492

The playwright Phrynichus is fined for upsetting the audience with his play, *The Fall of Miletus.*

490

The Athenians almost single-handedly defeat a large army of invading Persians at Marathon, northeast of Athens.

487

Comedies are officially recognized at the City Dionysia.

480

A united Greek fleet defeats the Persian fleet at Salamis, southwest of Athens; the following summer, an army made up of soldiers from many Greek city-states decisively defeats the Persian land army at Plataea, directly north of Athens; the Persians retire back into Asia, never to invade Europe again.

ca. 472

Aeschylus stages his historical tragedy, the *Persians,* which deals with the heroic Greek victory at Salamis.

ca. 470

Sophocles introduces the theatrical convention of the third actor.

468

Sophocles wins his first victory in the dramatic contests.

458

Aeschylus produces his Oresteia trilogy (the only Greek trilogy that has survived to the present).

ca. 450

The Athenian statesman Pericles initiates a fund to provide theater tickets to the poor.

ca. 447

Sophocles produces his *Ajax.*

ca. 441

Sophocles stages his *Antigone,* which draws on some of the same mythological material as Aeschylus's *Seven Against Thebes.*

431

The disastrous Peloponnesian War breaks out between the federations of city-states headed by Athens and Sparta and quickly engulfs much of the Greek world; Euripides produces his *Medea,* about a queen who murders her own children to achieve revenge against her husband.

ca. 429

Sophocles produces his *Oedipus the King,* which later ages will often call the greatest tragedy ever written.

428

Aristophanes produces his *Clouds.*

414

Aristophanes' *Birds* is first presented at the City Dionysia.

413

The Athenians suffer a debilitating blow as their expedition to capture the Greek city of Syracuse, in Sicily, meets with complete failure.

412

Euripides stages his *Helen.*

406

Sophocles writes *Oedipus at Colonus,* his sequel to *Oedipus the King,* and dies soon afterward.

404

Athens surrenders, ending the Peloponnesian War; for a short while, Athenian democracy is dismantled.

388

Aristophanes dies.

ca. 342–293

Life of the comic playwright Menander, chief exponent of what modern scholars call the New Comedy.

A.D.

1502–1518

The first modern printed versions of the surviving plays of Aeschylus, Sophocles, and Euripides appear in Italy and are rapidly translated into other European languages.

1585

Sophocles' *Oedipus the King* is first staged in an Italian theater.

1942

French playwright Jean Anouilh writes his famous modern version of Sophocles' *Antigone.*

1946

Famed English actor Laurence Olivier, widely regarded as the greatest actor of the twentieth century, plays Oedipus to wide acclaim at London's Old Vic Theater.

FOR FURTHER RESEARCH

GENERAL STUDIES OF ANCIENT GREEK DRAMA AND THEATER

James T. Allen, *Stage Antiquities of the Greeks and Romans and Their Influence*. New York: Cooper Square Publishers, 1963.

H.C. Baldry, *The Greek Tragic Theater*. New York: W.W. Norton, 1971.

Margarete Bieber, *The History of the Greek and Roman Theater*. Princeton: Princeton University Press, 1961.

Iris Brooke, *Costume in Greek Classic Drama*. London: Methuen, 1962.

James H. Butler, *The Theater and Drama of Greece and Rome*. San Francisco: Chandler Publishing, 1972.

Lionel Casson, *Masters of Ancient Comedy*. New York: Macmillan, 1960.

John Ferguson, *A Companion to Greek Tragedy*. Austin: University of Texas Press, 1972.

Marion Geisinger, *Plays, Players, and Playwrights: An Illustrated History of the Theater*. New York: Hart Publishing, 1971.

Karelisa V. Hartigan, *Greek Tragedy on the American Stage: Ancient Drama in the Commercial Theater, 1882–1994*. Westport, CT: Greenwood Press, 1995.

H.D.F. Kitto, *Greek Tragedy*. Garden City, NY: Doubleday, 1952.

Peter Levi, *A History of Greek Literature*. New York: Penguin Books, 1985.

D.W. Lucas, *The Greek Tragic Poets*. New York: W.W. Norton, 1959.

Don Nardo, *Greek and Roman Theater*. San Diego: Lucent Books, 1995.

Gilbert Norwood, *Greek Comedy.* New York: Hill and Wang, 1963.

———, *Greek Tragedy.* New York: Hill and Wang, 1960.

Arthur Pickard-Cambridge, *The Dramatic Festivals of Athens.* Oxford: Oxford University Press, 1968.

T.B.L. Webster, *Greek Theater Production.* London: Methuen, 1970.

ABOUT AESCHYLUS, SOPHOCLES, EURIPIDES, ARISTOPHANES, AND THEIR WORKS

Aristotle, *Poetics,* in Robert Maynard Hutchins, ed., *The Works of Aristotle,* in Great Books of the Western World Series. Chicago: Encyclopedia Britannica, 1952. Contains the philosopher's famous remarks about the origins of Greek theater and his critique of Greek drama.

William N. Bates, *Sophocles: Poet and Dramatist.* New York: Russell and Russell, 1969.

C.M. Bowra, *Sophoclean Tragedy.* Oxford: Clarendon Press, 1944.

K.J. Dover, *Aristophanic Comedy.* Berkeley: University of California Press, 1972.

G.M.A. Grube, *The Drama of Euripides.* New York: Barnes and Noble, 1961.

Bernard M.W. Knox, *The Heroic Temper: Studies in Sophoclean Tragedy.* Berkeley: University of California Press, 1966.

Don Nardo, ed., *Readings on Antigone.* San Diego: Greenhaven Press, 2000.

———, *Readings on Sophocles.* San Diego: Greenhaven Press, 1997.

T.G. Rosenmeyer, *The Art of Aeschylus.* Berkeley: University of California Press, 1982.

David Seale, *Vision and Stagecraft in Sophocles.* Chicago: University of Chicago Press, 1982.

T.A. Sinclair, *A History of Classical Greek Literature, from Homer to Aristotle.* New York: Haskell House, 1973.

Cedric H. Whitman, *Aristophanes and the Comic Hero.* Cambridge, MA: Harvard University Press, 1964.

For Further Research 168

————, *Sophocles: A Study of Heroic Humanism*. Cambridge, MA: Harvard University Press, 1951.

NOTABLE TRANSLATIONS OF CLASSIC GREEK PLAYS

Robert Fagles, trans., *Sophocles: The Three Theban Plays: Antigone, Oedipus the King, Oedipus at Colonus*. New York: Penguin Books, 1984.

David Grene and Richmond Lattimore, eds., *The Complete Greek Tragedies*. Chicago: University of Chicago Press, 1959.

Moses Hadas, ed., *The Complete Plays of Aristophanes*. New York: Bantam Books, 1962.

Stephen Halliwell, trans., *Aristophanes: Birds, Lysistrata, Assembly-Women, Wealth*. Oxford: Clarendon Press, 1997.

Rhoda A. Hendricks, ed. and trans., *Classical Gods and Heroes: Myths as Told by the Ancient Authors*. New York: Morrow Quill, 1974.

Richard C. Jebb, trans., *The Complete Plays of Sophocles*. New York: Bantam Books, 1967.

Bernard M.W. Knox, trans., *Oedipus the King*. New York: Pocket Books, 1959.

Paul Roche, trans., *The Orestes Plays of Aeschylus*. New York: New American Library, 1962.

Philip Vellacott, trans., *Aeschylus: Prometheus Bound, The Suppliants, Seven Against Thebes, The Persians*. Baltimore: Penguin Books, 1961.

————, trans., *Euripides: Medea and Other Plays*. New York: Penguin Books, 1963.

Rex Warner, trans., *Three Great Plays of Euripides*. New York: New American Library, 1958.

STUDIES OF ANCIENT GREEK SOCIETY AND CULTURE

Lesley Adkins and Roy A. Adkins, *Handbook to Life in Ancient Greece*. New York: Facts On File, 1997.

Sue Blundell, *Women in Ancient Greece*. Cambridge, MA: Harvard University Press, 1995.

C.M. Bowra, *Classical Greece*. New York: Time-Life Books, 1965.

————, *The Greek Experience*. New York: New American Library, 1957.

Michael Grant, *Myths of the Greeks and Romans.* New York: New American Library, 1962.

Edith Hamilton, *The Greek Way to Western Civilization.* New York: New American Library, 1942.

Victor D. Hanson, *The Western Way of War: Infantry Battle in Classical Greece.* New York: Oxford University Press, 1989.

Victor D. Hanson and John Heath, *Who Killed Homer? The Demise of Classical Education and the Recovery of Greek Wisdom.* New York: Free Press, 1998.

Robert B. Kebric, *Greek People.* Mountain View, CA: Mayfield Publishing, 1997.

Thomas R. Martin, *Ancient Greece: From Prehistoric to Hellenistic Times.* New Haven, CT: Yale University Press, 1996.

Don Nardo, *The Age of Pericles.* San Diego: Lucent Books, 1996.

——, *Greek and Roman Science.* San Diego: Lucent Books, 1997.

——, *Greek and Roman Sports.* San Diego: Lucent Books, 1999.

——, *Life in Ancient Athens.* San Diego: Lucent Books, 2000.

——, *The Parthenon.* San Diego: Lucent Books, 1999.

——, *The Trial of Socrates.* San Diego: Lucent Books, 1997.

Sarah B. Pomeroy, *Goddesses, Whores, Wives, and Slaves: Women in Classical Antiquity.* New York: Shocken Books, 1995.

Sarah B. Pomeroy et al., *Ancient Greece: A Political, Social, and Cultural History.* New York: Oxford University Press, 1999.

Jacqueline de Romilly, *A Short History of Greek Literature.* Trans. Lillian Doherty. Chicago: University of Chicago Press, 1985.

Nigel Spivey, *Greek Art.* London: Phaidon Press, 1997.

Chester G. Starr, *The Ancient Greeks.* New York: Oxford University Press, 1971.

Alfred Zimmern, *The Greek Commonwealth.* New York: Modern Library, 1931.

INDEX